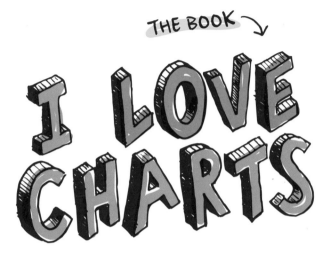

THE BOOK

I LOVE CHARTS

Jason Oberholtzer and Cody Westphal

Foreword by David Karp, founder of Tumblr, Inc.

sourcebooks

Published by Sourcebooks, Inc.
P.O. Box 4410, Naperville, Illinois 60567-4410
(630) 961-3900
Fax: (630) 961-2168
www.sourcebooks.com

Library of Congress Cataloging-in-Publication Data

Oberholtzer, Jason.
 I love charts : the book / Jason Oberholtzer and Cody Westphal.
    p. cm.
 1. Popular culture—Humor. 2. Charts, diagrams, etc.—Humor. I. Westphal,
Cody. II. Title.
 PN6231.P635O24 2012
 818'.602—dc23
                    2012007166

Printed and bound in the United States of America.
VP 10 9 8 7 6 5 4 3 2 1

Contents

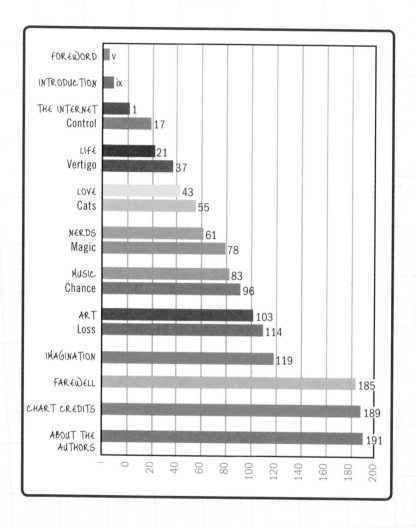

FOREWORD	v
INTRODUCTION	ix
THE INTERNET	1
Control	17
LIFE	21
Vertigo	37
LOVE	43
Cats	55
NERDS	61
Magic	78
MUSIC	83
Chance	96
ART	103
Loss	114
IMAGINATION	119
FAREWELL	185
CHART CREDITS	189
ABOUT THE AUTHORS	191

FOREWORD

I STARTED FOLLOWING THE *I Love Charts* blog on February 20th, 2010, the day they posted this Valentine Venn Diagram.

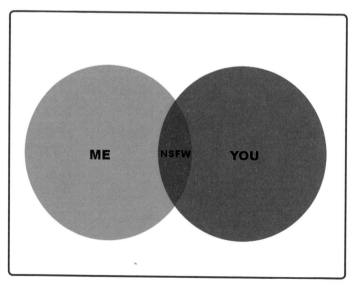

I'm probably a much bigger nerd than I realize for thinking these circles are sweet, but it's certainly not the first time I've been moved by a chart.

As I'm neither a talented writer nor a confident speaker, I've always leaned on carefully designed charts and images to get my point across. This was very much the inspiration for Tumblr. It seemed so unfair that I couldn't *blog* my thoughts or discoveries just because I didn't have the wherewithal to hammer out paragraphs of text. Tumblr offered an alternative where those subjects could be concisely presented in their purest form—an image, a quote, a thought without context. No editorial voice.

And that, perhaps, is why I share Jason and Cody's love for this art form. Charts present information succinctly. But they do more than that. In the right hands, they can just as quickly make you laugh or lament. The charts in the following chapters do everything from parody life on earth to share heartfelt moments of love and loss. Jason and Cody prove that with their distinct editorial voice, charts can become something even more illuminating and personal than I had imagined possible.

The *I Love Charts* blog has always succeeded thanks to the willingness of Jason and Cody to let their personalities shine through. The blog would have done fine as a bunch of silly charts, but instead has become one of the most visible and influential blogs on Tumblr by reflecting the interests and sensibilities of its founders. This book does that and then some. In addition to a collection of humorous and interesting charts, this book is full of extraordinary writing, full of insight and candor.

Jason and Cody's examination of this form also does a wonderful job of paying homage to the brilliant chartists out there. Many of the charts you will see here are not the work of the authors, but of a community of relentlessly talented contributors. The creations posted every day are giving life to an entirely new art form.

Simply put, I love charts.

David Karp
Founder
Tumblr, Inc.

INTRODUCTION

YES, WE ARE AWARE that chart is not in color. Welcome to *I Love Charts: The Book*.

Charts are invaluable tools for communication. At their best, they display data in a way that gives it character and emotional resonance, that tells the story behind the numbers. Charts can facilitate learning and influence opinions, can illuminate simple truths and recontextualize conversations. Charts are so versatile you can display almost anything with them, which is not necessarily a good thing.

With charts, like with any tool, there is a risk of becoming overly dependent on common usage, constrained by rules and hedged in by habit. One can end up forgetting the original purpose of both the tool and its wielder. A good chart has to serve a function while conveying that function's

Data

Information

Presentation

Knowledge

EpicGraphic.com

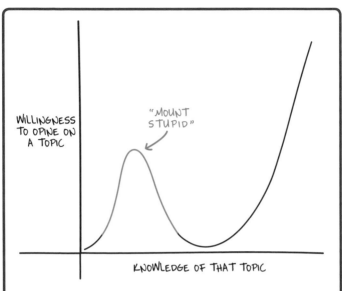

Phrases uttered atop Mount Stupid:

- *"Historically, the Amazons would cut off their right breast so they could shoot a bow and arrow."*

- *"The American Civil War really had nothing to do with slavery."*

- *"Biologically, the tomato is a fruit, not a vegetable."*

- 99% of phrases that start with *"Now, I don't know much about quantum physics, BUT—"*

importance. While the function is often the clear presentation of quantitative data, the charts that interest us the most endeavor to do something more personal, to display qualitative data in a quantitative manner. Those are the charts you will find in this book.

See, we chose not to color in the first chart for a reason very dear to us. We have things to say and we want you to pay attention. They may not be very important things, but we will let you decide. While we respect grand anthologies of quantitative data exhaustively researched and masterfully displayed, this will not be one of those books. We are more interested in the relationship between the quantitative and the qualitative, and the stories that arise from that relationship.

So that's what we are going to give you: stories. Stories about charts. Stories told with the aid of charts. Stories told as essays, anecdotes, asides, quips, loose observations, and generalities.

What qualifies us to write such a book? The sheer volume and inertia of our hubris, that's what. We have seen tens of thousands of charts, which at least puts us comfortably atop Mount Stupid. And from that summit we shall preach!

If that's not enough to convince you that we are qualified to write this book, may we now direct your attention to our undeniably, overwhelmingly moderate Internet fame. Taking a look at this chart over here, I can assure you we weigh in somewhere between S- and M-list celebrities, with a compelling case to be made for the P-list (I know we promised you stories, but you are not getting that one, sorry).

Rank of Celebrity

LIST	Description
A	Multi-million dollars per film/television appearance
B	Standout in ensemble TV medical or crime drama / star of a premium cable series
C	Appear as walk-on cameo in latest Apatow movie / "that guy"
D	Supporting actor in sitcom (annoying voice, marginal catch phrase)
E	Major sport professional athlete (non-endorser, non-NHL) / Reader of nominees at awards ceremony, does not open envelope
F	Reality show contestant (elimination format, top 10)
G	Former child actor, possible sketchy legal history
H	Porn star with last name / Actor on Nickelodeon or Disney Channel series, non-starring.
I	Cable news talking head, basic cable home repair show host
J	Olympic athlete (non-gold medal winner)
K	Had intimate details of your sex life revealed on internet
L	Reality dating show contestant
M	Star of memorable regional cable commercial (see Eddie, Crazy)
N	Local sports hero / State senator
O	Had a police composite sketch of yourself appear on local news
P	Had intercourse with an NBA player
Q	Shticky beer/hot dog vendor at sports arena
R	"Guide" on theme park adventure ride
S	Once retweeted by celebrity. Noticed misspelling in original post after the fact.
T	Held a sign behind Matt Lauer's head on *The Today Show*
U	You were waiting in line to use a pay phone and the guy who was on the phone turns around and it was Emilio Estevez. The *Mighty Ducks* man. I swear to God. I was there.
V	You pay $40 to have a poem published in a book of poetry (see also International Star Registry)
W	Your name appeared in a local news story about a "mysterious sighting." Name misspelled on chyron
X	The people you call your friends all call you by your WoW handle
Y	People you know would let you go a whole day with a piece of food on your face
Z	You could die in your house and it would take anyone years to notice

Not impressed by our celebrity status? Well perhaps it is the wide network of talented and generous friends we have come across in our rise to moderate celebrity that qualifies us to write this book. We have had the pleasure of working with some of brightest, most dedicated minds on the Internet, many of whom we have enlisted to fill our book with wonderful, original charts for us to riff off of—luminaries

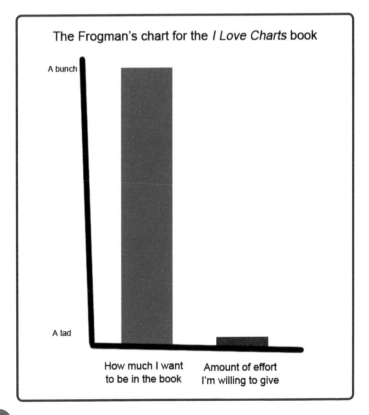

The Frogman's chart for the *I Love Charts* book

A bunch

A tad

How much I want to be in the book

Amount of effort I'm willing to give

like Ben Grelle, or as the Internet knows him, The Frogman, who when asked to contribute said he had the perfect chart for us and...oof. Thanks a lot, Ben.

I'd like to think that what qualifies us to write the book goes beyond our incredibly er...helpful group of Internet friends. It has something to do with that magical word, which is enjoying something of an extended renaissance—curation. Yes, we are curators. And yes, that is often just a fancy word for bloggers, which is often just a fancy word for unemployed writers, which is often just a fancy word for drunks. But in this case, it is all that, minus the unemployed part! We believe in careful curation, giving great work and talented people their due, and above all, pith.

We hope you enjoy our book.

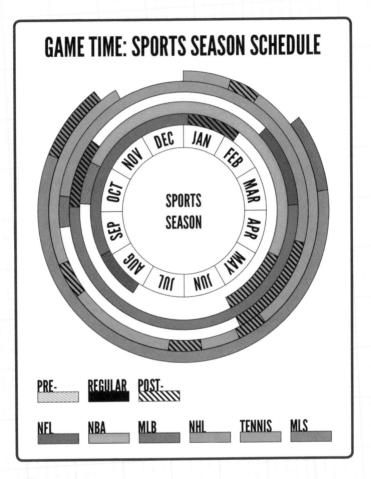

Before we get started in earnest, we thought we would give you a starting-the-book present in the form of this handy year-round sports season chart. Don't say we've never done anything for you.

I Love Charts

THE INTERNET

YES, THIS BOOK "COMES from the Internet"; let's just get that out of the way. There is a stigma attached to the book born of the Internet, as if topics that flourish online inherently lack the proper profundity for the printed word. Worse, hidden behind the judgment of subject matter is the elitist insinuation that writers who find success on the Internet are less talented and less deserving of their success. There is an intimation that these writers are sojourners in the public consciousness, a consciousness of which books are an acceptably canonical reflection, since they too inhabit the "real word," but which largely excludes literature of the Internet, a "fake world."

Luckily for us, this perception is changing, thanks to (1) an increasing number of the Internet's most talented denizens finding success through traditional publishing, and (2) the increasing reliance of traditional media on the

Internet to publish content. Of course this is good for us professionally, because we are writing a book based on a website, but it is also good for me personally, because I recently realized I've lost track of the line where the Internet ends and life outside the Internet begins. Where once there was clearly "Internet life" and "real life," and distinct personalities to go with each, now there is just Jason, some sort of early model cyborg.

As the Internet becomes a larger part of our social, cultural, and vocational lives, we are forced to make choices about the extent to which we are willing to embrace the medium and its native relationships and emotions. There is often a temptation (from which I am not immune) to discredit the authenticity of an experience on the Internet, but to do so is a waste of time. That is not to say that understanding the cause of an emotion or the foundation of an experience is not valuable (there are few more worthwhile pursuits in my neurotic opinion), but it is to say that discrediting an emotion's existence because of its source is just plain dumb. People fall in love on the Internet. People fight on the Internet. People create communities more meaningful than the communities they can interact with physically. That is all old news.

TOO MUCH TIME ONLINE

©www.googlygooeys.com, 2011.

The Internet 3

What is newer news is the way in which people are allowing their relationships online to spill offline, and vice versa. Relationships of every nature, from romantic to casual, are being enriched by the combination of online and offline personas. But even this news is not that new.

What may be new is the increasing number of people, myself included, who see no difference between online and offline life. There is no point at which one ends and the other begins. Maybe I am just an Internet person and this is just what happens when you turn twenty-five and settle into your personality. Maybe none of this is remarkable, but it seems like more is going on.

The Internet is the only place to which I feel truly nationalistic and is the environment in which I feel most at home. You know what is odd about that? Mostly that it is no longer odd. There are now young adults who have had a significant portion of their foundational life experiences online. And from all generations, people spend more time on their computers than ever before; some spend more time on them than off them, especially if you include tablets and smartphones. When the Internet was more of a diversion, or a tool for the few, it made more sense to deride it as "fake life," but now it encompasses too much for that classification to stick. So why not treat the Internet as an equal part of your life? Whether or not you consider your involvement with the

Internet to be as extreme as mine, it affects you every single day. Why not treat it with the respect it deserves?

Like it or not, the majority of modern relationships involve the Internet. We use the Internet for meeting, courting, networking, catching up, stalking, or broadcasting shared experiences. Your very framework of social etiquette has adapted to accommodate the Internet. The volume of minute interpersonal decisions you make every day (usually subconsciously) has expanded.

Matters of email and Twitter etiquette can now be codified. They make or break relationships. I'm sure there are people who find that ridiculous, but deal with it! Acting holier-than-thou on matters of Internet etiquette is little

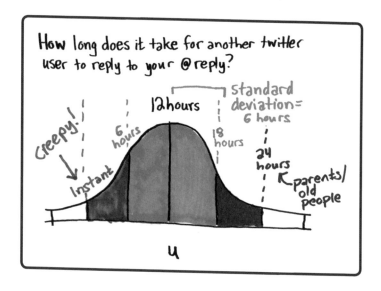

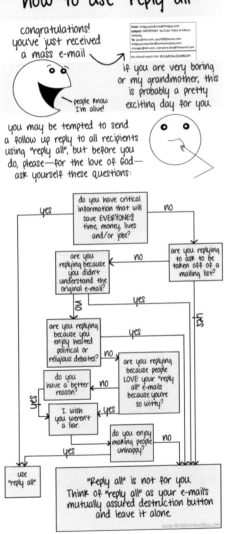

I Love Charts

more than a disguise for laziness or fear. Who cares where your social life plays out? Ultimately it's all just playing out in your head anyway, so why scoff at how it gets there?

Pay attention and put some care into your online correspondences. Speaking the lingo isn't about embracing tech-speak, it's about communicating with people. Just because you are communicating with somebody via the Internet doesn't mean you should care less about how it turns out.

So I guess what I am saying is have some pride in your Internet persona; it is just as real as your offline persona. You don't have to go as far as I have and discard all boundaries in the search for some true cross-platform cyborg self, but you shouldn't be afraid to invest yourself online. Treat the Internet like a real space and you will be rewarded...by turning into a mildly agoraphobic recluse like me.

By the way, that is another misguided stereotype. Having a healthy relationship with the Internet does not necessarily mean you will turn into an agoraphobe. Rather, you are turning into an agoraphobe because the world is a horrifying place!

The relationships formed on the Internet are not just interpersonal. Institutions have been personalized so much through social media that Corporate Personhood might not (in this regard and this regard alone) be that inaccurate a classification. Facebook comes to mind. People actually love this service, which is evident by how much people

profess to hate this service. There is real emotion there, significant engagement with a company. People are willing to trust Facebook with all their most personal information and yet do not trust them to pull off a redesign without it being the end of the world. That new thing they did that you were complaining about—you have already adapted to it.

It is no accident that the trend of humanizing institutions, and the expectations we have developed for their transparency, have served as the prelude for a period of vast and vocal populist sentiment. The more access one has to the people who make up an institution, the more value those people hold and the more approachable and accountable the institution becomes. All the individuality the Internet promotes, so often derided as a me-first culture, has allowed us to appreciate the importance of the individual and, in so doing, has thrown a wrench into traditional employer-employee relations. The ever-important question is: Who is really doing whom a favor?

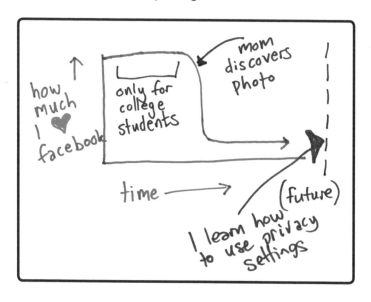

When a situation is boiled down to the people involved, and those people are treated equally, things can get complicated. Well, the Internet complicates almost everything it touches—access to information tends to do that.

HOW TO DO A RESEARCH PAPER
1990
2010
GO TO THE LIBRARY
FIND BOOKS USING THE DEWEY DECIMAL SYSTEM
BOOK IS ALREADY CHECKED OUT
WAIT UNTIL BOOK IS RETURNED
RETURN HOME WITH BOOK AND BREAKOUT THE TYPEWRITER
TYPE A LITTLE
MESS UP
ATTEMPT TO FIX MISTAKES WITH WHITE OUT
ANGER
DEPRESSION
SUICIDE
DONE!
GO TO WIKIPEDIA
REGURGITATE INFORMATION
DONE!
SUICIDE
PILLS
GUN
DONE!
endlessorigami.blogspot.com

It's not just philosophically that the Internet has changed what it means to be a modern worker. Getting down to the nuts and bolts of getting work done, the Internet has made another mess of things. It has simultaneously made us more and less productive. The entire work process has changed at all levels, from professional to academic.

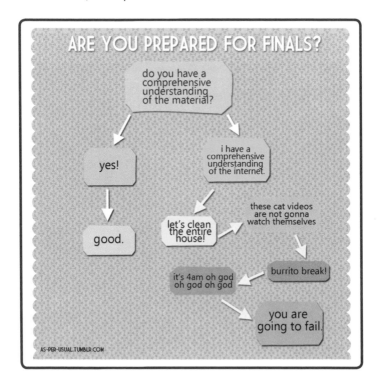

The access to tools and information the Internet provides may not have been the best thing for workers. Increased productivity usually benefits those who employ the increasingly productive more than those paid to work more quickly. Today's worker is expected to cover a lot of ground. What's worse, they have to do so while constantly logged on to the greatest tool for distraction and procrastination ever invented! Oh yeah, and they get paid less.

I Love Charts

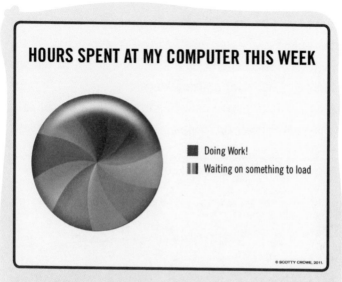

HOURS SPENT AT MY COMPUTER THIS WEEK

■ Doing Work!

❚❚❚ Waiting on something to load

© SCOTTY CROWE, 2011.

CODY'S QUIP

THE INTERNET: The best and worst thing to happen to getting projects finished since

With work and play and love and hate and everything else all on the same screen, free time and work time are blurring. The less we segment and compartmentalize, the more we are forced to confront important gray areas in our relationships (with people and institutions) that have always been present but now are easier to isolate. When is an employee not an employee and to what extent do his decisions reflect his employer? What should be public and what should be private? What right does somebody have to their online space and who has the right to police it? How much time can I spend on a stranger's social media sites before it qualifies as stalking them?

What I find most interesting is somebody's right to his or her own online privacy vis-à-vis their employer. Is it fair to

measure suitability for employment by the thoughts, opinions, and actions that exist in a space that, while public, is clearly marked as one's personal space? To me, responsible conduct on the Internet is less about how best to remain employable and more about managing your social media presence such that it is an accurate and comprehensive portrayal of you, a human being. I choose to try to be as transparent as possible, online and offline, and I hope that

I Love Charts

effort is appreciated and respected, not just used in some bogus armchair employment psychology.

Ultimately I think transparency is always a better option, especially now that we have tools that make it so easy to share our interests and opinions. Why not be the whole of your person at all times, online and off, with your boss and with your friends? It's more accurate to the human experience, and I think we are capable of handling it. It's better than holing up and walling off everything we care about with privacy restrictions and circles within circles. The Internet

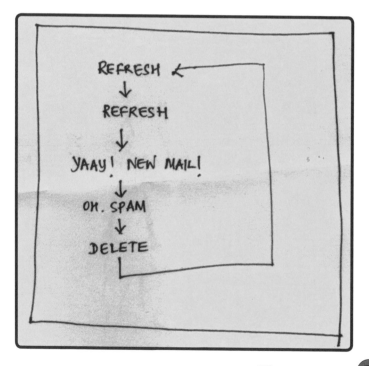

thrives on hope, not on fear and limitations. Great things can be found by venturing out into the noise and hoping to find something...fulfilling. Be your aims social, professional, or academic, the Internet is a great big mess of hope and disappointment, and that is why I am proud to say this book "comes from the Internet."

I Love Charts

CONTROL

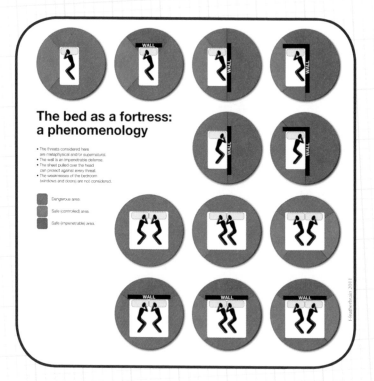

The bed as a fortress: a phenomenology

- The threats considered here are metaphysical and/or supernatural.
- The wall is an impenetrable defense.
- The sheet pulled over the head can protect against every threat.
- The weaknesses of the bedroom (windows and doors) are not considered.

Dangerous area.

Safe (controlled) area.

Safe (impenetrable) area.

Heatherbrain 2011

From as young as I can remember until an age probably a few years past when it turns embarrassing, this was still my practice: I slept with my head under the blankets, a hole exposed at my mouth to let in air. The size of the hole would depend on how brave I was feeling that night, ranging from a pin-prick that was likely a suffocation risk to an opening encircling my face.

It was recently brought to my attention by my mother that there remains in me a vestige of this behavior. When I am beginning to get sick—before I can detect the tickle on the back of my throat, before my eyes start to get sensitive to light, before I notice a dip in my energy level—I make a subconscious choice to dress for the occasion, wrap a blanket around my head, and walk around the house looking very much like the Virgin Mary from a nativity scene. I've learned to catch myself doing this, because the headdress means, without fail, that within twenty-four hours I will be in bed with a nasty cold or the flu.

The worst nightmares I had when I was a child involved mannequins. They would come in through my bedroom window or up the stairs and through my door and would tickle me until it was painful. I would laugh until I gasped and my sides hurt from both the laughter and the jabbing of their hands. I would plead with them to stop, scream at their smooth, white, featureless faces. Ultimately, I would do one of three things: break their grasp and run out of my house, wake up, or "wake up." The worst option was "waking up," a cruel trick my mind learned to play on me once it realized I was developing too

I Love Charts

many tools to deal with the nightmares it decided I needed to have in order to sort out...whatever it is nightmares are there to help children sort out.

"Waking up" was a move my mind developed as a reaction to my hard-won ability to lucid dream. When in the course of a nightmare I realized I was dreaming, I would frantically try to isolate the muscles that controlled my (real) eyes and force them open. Once I found the muscles, I could connect them to my eyes in the dream and would push at them, though it felt like they were held together by tar. Isolating the muscles was not enough; there are other obstacles the dreaming body puts in the way of your dream actions becoming physical actions, so I would keep pushing and focusing on my (real) eyes until my face ached, usually while running from mannequins.

I would push and push and then finally, I would see a crack of light, my consciousness would shift, and my eyes would slowly open, revealing my room before me. I was lying in my bed. I was safe.

I would get out of my bed, walk to my bedroom door, open it, and through that door would rush the mute army of mannequins once again, pinning me to the bed, jabbing my sides. Thrashing, I would refocus on my eyes, vowing to *really* open them this time, to not be tricked. Moments of agony passed and then the hands would vanish and I would again be in my bed. The room looked more clear this time. The sun was out. The door flew open.

As the mannequins charged at me, I would gather all my energy and focus it at the top of my head, begging for control over my thoughts again, imagining my consciousness as Drano bubbles, coursing through my skull and cleaning out foreign agents. My eyes would open and everything would be dark.

* * *

I only realize I'm nervous for something if I wake up on the morning that it's supposed to happen hungover. I've made more difficult for myself a number of trips, deadlines, performances, and romantic encounters because of this. There is no mystery here; drinking to reduce anxiety or stress is a fairly common occurrence. However, I do wish that I could train myself to sense the desire of my shoulders for relaxation, the quickness of my face to flush, the unwarranted confidence of my steps, and realize, before the pounding head the next morning, that the events of the day to come mean more to me than I want to admit.

* * *

Sometimes, when trying to conjure a particular phrase, definition, or memory that is eluding me, I am struck by how very unfair it is that I have so much available in my brain and so little control over any of it.

—Jason

I Love Charts

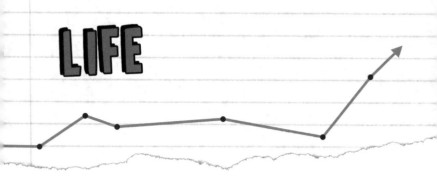

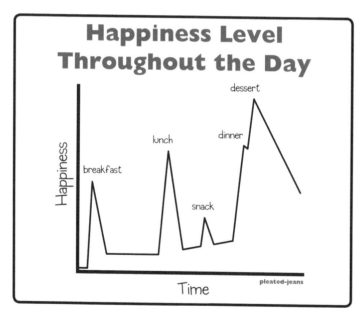

IT IS AN ABSOLUTE mystery to me what is required for me to stay productive. I do, however, know that happiness is involved somehow, though the relationship is mercurial. There is a perfect balance of comfort and discomfort that allows me to do creative work, and I am constantly either trying to find the mix or capitalize on it when the mix finds me.

There are times I cannot get any good work done until I have managed to make myself miserable to some degree by forgoing sleep, skipping meals, and managing my time poorly. On these occasions, exhaustion, anxiety, and anomie form the adrenaline needed for me to focus. To be clear, absolutely none of this is healthy and I do not recommend it, but for whatever reason it works.

There are other times when the behavior described above robs me of any ability to get good work done and leaves me very close to deadlines, still searching for ways to rein my head in and get done what needs to get done. The majority of time in whatever counts as my work process is spent trying to wrangle my attention, which I either lack the discipline or understanding to consistently manage in ways better for my health.

There are times when feeling excited or motivated can keep me productive and produce good results. There are times when being excited or motivated fragments my attention past any usefulness. There are times when being content means a steady stream of work. There are times when it means a steady stream of mediocrity.

Are my work habits somehow a necessary part of my productivity or are they just bad work habits? I suspect it is a bit of column A, a bit of column B, and a whole lot of column C, which involves other variables seemingly unrelated to the tasks at hand.

So what does this have to do with anything? Well, when analyzing proclivities, particularly those you wish you could change, most fall, in some distribution, across those same three columns: (1) You are doing something because it works to some extent; (2) You are doing something poorly that you could change; or (3) Your actions are connected to other variables, like general happiness. The first column is best to accept; you have found something that works and for now, that is fine. The second column is where most of the guilt comes from, but is often hard to fix without first

addressing the third column. The third column is why I have lately been treating happiness like a commodity.

When you work from home, as I have for more than a year now, you learn how to motivate yourself. Sure, you have to do that for any job, but working from home, you take on the role of your own boss, coworker, confidant, and competition. Since your physical location varies very little (especially in the winter), the various parts of your day lose their definition and compartmentalization becomes difficult. Connections between all your actions, all that you consume, and your mental well-being become clearer. You start to notice things like "I can't do a single bit of work for at least 15 minutes after I shower" and "this leftover pizza will make me feel dumb." It can make you feel like a factory, fueled by happiness, the product of which is "work."

People wonder why public discourse has become so combative and dehumanized. In the course of these first two chapters I have compared myself to both a cyborg and a factory. Hang in there, we talk about cats later.

I'm having trouble focusing. Snack? Meal? New chair? Couch? Bed? Break to read something? Break to watch something? Shower? New room? Switch projects? Double down on this one? Caffeine? Booze? Sleep? More light? Less light? Music? Silence? Take a walk? Lay down? Concentrate on something challenging? On something dumb? More clothes? Less clothes? No clothes?

I am twenty-five years old, which seems to be right at the beginning of a transitional period. A lot of my peers are, for the first time, in positions where they feel happy and like they have a purpose. Whether it's because they have been somewhere long enough to get out of the entry ranks, found the field they want to be pursuing, decided to go back to school, or have finally gotten out of school, it seems like my peers are finding niches where they can be happy and pursue a vision of success that makes sense to them.

This is encouraging, because for most people I know it was far from an easy journey to get to a place of moderate satisfaction. However, for every person I know who seems to be settling into this transitional period, there are many I know who are still struggling to find direction.

Part of the joy of curating a website that has a large stream of user-generated content is that you get to know your audience fairly intimately. If I had to describe the most typical outlook I see from the members of our audience who are around my age, it would look something like this chart.

This chart is a bit hyperbolic, but I know a lot of people (many of whom send me charts similar to these) who genuinely look to the future with a mixture of resignation and despair—though of course, my generation being what it is,

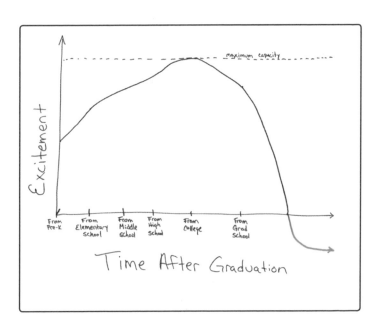

I Love Charts

there is a healthy dose of irony and self-deprecation included. It all does seem a bit heavy on the doom and gloom, but the data is in and the model is very consistent. Most people have a rough go of it in their twenties and send us charts to prove it.

However, there is a sense of optimism hiding in all the irony. Continuing to speak in generalities, my generation seems to have an attitude where they are willing to struggle if it means they get to pursue the opportunities which interest them, and are willing to give up some money early on and spend some time feeling lost and depressed while they figure things out. Of course, we say this is our idea, but the whole lack of jobs thing probably had a hand in that.

I promised you stories, so here goes—a whole lot of qualitative, with a backbone of solid data. I said we've seen more than 10,000 charts; well a good 1,000 could probably fit in this story line. Extrapolated from more than two years of user-generated content, this is the story of the archetypal *I Love Charts* millennial reader.

First, you graduate from college in the spring of some year between 2002 and 2010 and spend the summer trying to find work. By fall, work being hard to find, you end up with either no job, something that doesn't pay, or something part time. Regardless, you are "in the real world" now, so you have much to learn. Your fall schedule ends up looking something like this.

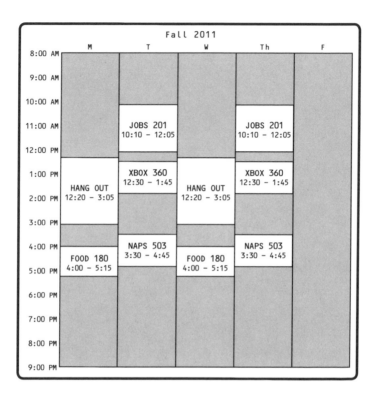

Fall 2011

	M	T	W	Th	F
8:00 AM					
9:00 AM					
10:00 AM					
11:00 AM		JOBS 201 10:10 – 12:05		JOBS 201 10:10 – 12:05	
12:00 PM					
1:00 PM	HANG OUT 12:20 – 3:05	XBOX 360 12:30 – 1:45	HANG OUT 12:20 – 3:05	XBOX 360 12:30 – 1:45	
2:00 PM					
3:00 PM					
4:00 PM	FOOD 180 4:00 – 5:15	NAPS 503 3:30 – 4:45	FOOD 180 4:00 – 5:15	NAPS 503 3:30 – 4:45	
5:00 PM					
6:00 PM					
7:00 PM					
8:00 PM					
9:00 PM					

Sooner or later, through perseverance (read: luck, nepotism, or a willingness to have worked for free for an extended period of time), you find yourself gainfully employed. At this point, you realize you suck at your job. You are not suited for this at all and have no idea how you got here. You feel like a fraud.

After spending a few months constantly on the verge of panic attacks, worried your ignorance will be exposed, you realize that nobody knows what they are doing. Everybody

I Love Charts

at every level in business is bluffing most of the time, and your ignorance is in good company. Your general anxiety dips, but you realize you still are not happy at your job. You start to believe that your experience in the "real world" has allowed you to hone enough skills to make you qualified for a job you would prefer. You look around and realize that all the jobs that interest you pay next to nothing. You apply for those jobs, but also for positions that seem boring and for which you consider yourself overqualified. Why? Because they pay a lot more. They will be just like safety schools—you will definitely get an offer (remember all those skills you are pretty sure you have now?), and they will try to lure you with better financial packages.

You are qualified for none of the jobs you applied for. Nobody hires you. Most don't even respond to you. You stay working at the same place and apathy starts to

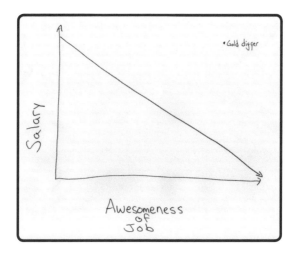

creep in. What went wrong? You couldn't even get an inter-view to display all these skills you are pretty sure you have. Nobody would look past the lack of experience. You start to ponder the age-old paradox of how one gets the experi-ence to qualify for entry-level positions if one can't get an entry-level position (due to lack of experience) needed to gain experience.

Well, now you have to prove that you can stay some-where long enough to get up to that magical "three years of experience" level so you can apply to more jobs. So, you have to stay put. You are not thrilled about this.

Notice, though, the chunk of the following pie chart ded-icated to "dreaming about the wonderful things to come." It is this segment that makes possible your survival during the

I Love Charts

"gaining experience to hit the arbitrary three years mark" part of your life. It is also this segment that allows you to test your limits and the possibilities of your mind, while your physical surroundings fail to do so. Your dreaming becomes less about escapism and more about possibilities—intellectual, emotional, logistical possibilities. You start seeing your options differently, though mostly in the form of a dream.

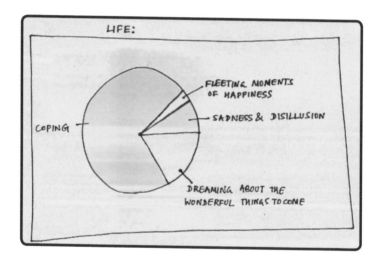

One day, you realize you actually have accumulated the experience needed to move on in your career, but that your experience has nothing to do with the job you were tasked to do. The experience you gained was from the time in your head, dreaming in opposition to your surroundings, creating hypotheses for your life and following them to their logical

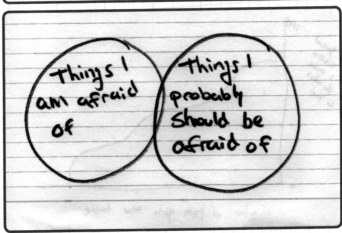

I Love Charts

conclusions. You have no idea what to do to make yourself happy or what you want to do with your life, but you know now that the most important thing, what you want more than anything else, is agency. You want to be an adult. The only thing holding you back is fear.

So, you break from your experience-accumulation plan and go toward what you feel will make you happier, even if the process is more like dowsing than using GPS. The decision doesn't feel perfect, but it feels better, and that is enough to make you work harder.

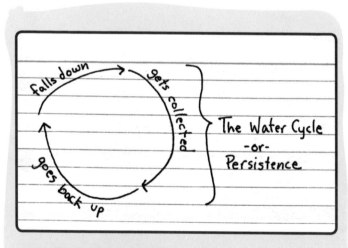

CODY QUIP

That's some tubthumpingly good advice.

You realize at some point that you are working harder than you ever thought you could and that while spending three years at a job you hated would only marginally have changed your skill-set, spending just a few months caring about what you do and fighting for some vague promise of purpose have completely changed you. You find reserves of energy only used previously in particularly trying relationships. Productivity isn't business speak, it is a lifestyle.

As your work becomes part of you, it manifests itself in some tangible skill. You realize you are now actually good at something. The skill has less to do with lessons from your work and more to do with knowledge about yourself. Your time spent challenging yourself, fighting for agency, and caring about the outcome has rewarded you with a better sense of yourself and your capabilities.

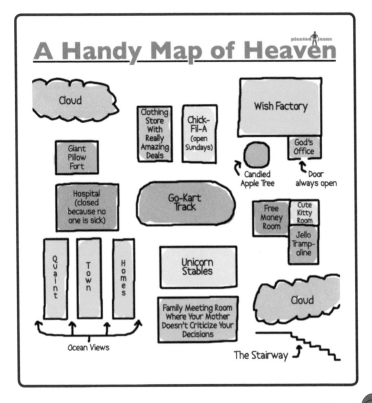

You take your skill and your work ethic and go back into the world: to school, to a new field, to try your hand at freelancing. You feel for the first time that you have direction, which came from dreams and grew to an interest, to a skill, to an application of that skill. Things might not be so bad. The challenges are just beginning, you are broke, and the economy is horrible, but at least you know what you want to be doing (if only for the moment). Now that you have this life thing figured out, all that is left to worry about is death.

A Handy Map of Hell

I Love Charts

VERTIGO

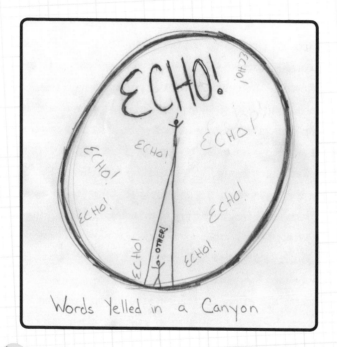

Words Yelled in a Canyon

When I was young, let's say in the eight-to-twelve range, I took a tour of Ford's Theatre. I don't remember much, but I do remember thinking, as I looked out from the box in which Lincoln was shot, that John Wilkes Booth was a weakling for having injured his leg in his leap from the box to the stage. It didn't look like so bad a fall. I visualized over and over again making the leap, landing on my feet just long enough to tip my momentum into a forward roll, and taking that momentum into a sprint for the door. It was so simple. Your physical limitations are all a matter of a lack of planning. I could isolate each muscle it would take, imagine each spin of my arms to maintain balance during the fall. Jump—two or three spins of my arms—feet down—bend knees, tip into roll—pop up with my shoulder—pull my head back as I begin my sprint to correct balance. That's how to kill a president and get away with class.

The tour guide moved us out of the box and toward the Petersen House museum. He was speaking, but I couldn't pay attention. All I wanted to do was try that jump. Each step down the stairs from the balcony level brought a new surge of adrenaline. I was losing my chance. I wanted this jump. My body wanted this jump. Each muscle was ready to perform its function in this feat of dexterity. I was shaking. Jumping was my only hope for catharsis.

I came out of my adrenaline haze in the Petersen House museum, looking through glass at a piece of cloth stained with Lincoln's blood. I believe it was cut from his shirt as they operated on him. There were other, more interesting items in the museum (including the rest of his iconic outfit) but this is the only item I remember. I stared at that small strip of cloth with an intensity I knew I had to hide. I walked elsewhere and

I Love Charts

returned, wandered the room while keeping the strip of cloth in the corner of my eye.

Whenever I see a woman I fear I might fall in love with, or a Van Gogh painting, I treat them the same way I treated that spot of blood. I refuse to look at them straight on when I think other people are looking at me. When I think I am unobserved, I look until I blush and have to scurry to another part of the room.

To be honest, I'm not sure I ever stood in the box in which Lincoln was shot. I'm not sure if you are allowed to. I suspect I might have stood in one adjacent. However, I know what it feels like to jump from that box more than anybody possibly can who has never done so.

* * *

I took a day trip to Boston at around the same age as my experience at Ford Theatre. My family and I drove up from Glastonbury, Connecticut, to do...I have no idea what. I came home with two rolls of film taken with the first camera I had ever owned. These were among the first few roles I ever shot. The roles contained nothing but the graves of famous figures from American history. Hancock, Adams, Revere, more. The last few shots on the second roll were taken out the window of the car as we drove back to Connecticut, blurry buildings on the side of the Mass Pike.

* * *

I stood on the balcony of a friend's ninth-floor apartment in Boston last summer and talked about jumping. He had just finished convincing me that The Beatles would have been less successful with John Bonham as their drummer, so in return, I was convincing him that I knew why people put in high places think about the logistics of jumping, or why there exists that moment when, driving windy back roads at night, we are hit with the realization that it is within our power to put our bumper full speed into the nearest tree, or why we do advanced physics and why our legs tense when the train we are waiting for approaches.

"It comes down to power," I told him. "At this moment, we face a choice. We have the power to effect great change immediately, but at the expense of the future. Let's look at it as a gamble. There is before me an option to do something with immediate and enormous repercussions. It will impact the world, or at least my corner of it, more than any other action I have available to me at the moment. There will be the outpouring of grief, the hurt, the questions. The impact of my time alive will be clear, as it is defined by the legacy of my death. It is instant access to meaning, right there in front of me. Therefore, all morality of the decision aside, every time I don't jump, I am choosing to believe that this sudden conclusion is not worth it. I'm betting that the aggregate impact of my life will be greater than the impact of ending it. And this has nothing to do with happiness or sadness or anything that took place before the

I Love Charts

moment I reached this railing. This is just being aware of your options, even when doing so makes you flinch. And it is more my body, driven by something primitive, that recognizes the options, that recoils even while advancing, drawn as to a Siren to…something. I'm not quite sure what. Okay, now we can pull morality back into it, at least as it pertains to my responsibility to other people. It's not guilt that makes us think of others in this moment, nor is it some abstract morality. It is a gaze down at our chips. We count all those people we know, who we care about, who we love. We count our intellectual endeavors, the questions we want to answer. We count everything we know to be beautiful, all our aesthetic goals. We count all the mysteries that would end. We do this all in an instant and mash it all together into a sense of self. Here is what we have to wager. We then look to the future and weigh the unknown. We know there will be struggle and pain and sorrow and loss, because ultimately that one certainty in life vibrates through all previous events. We do not know what will happen to us or what our lives will mean in spite of this certainty. The same vivid imagination that is currently running through a checklist of muscles and driving my adrenaline, as I place my hand on this railing, takes our sense of self, then draws either from memories or predictions, from dreams, from art, from that primitive place, and creates for itself a home, right in the pits of our stomachs, where it can iterate. The future is born in our stomachs. Multiple futures. Visceral possibilities. And when this happens, I can't help it, and I fall in love with the future. I have no evidence that the pros will outweigh the cons; I can't point to anything that suggests I will make an impact that I can intellectually stack up against the power I have at this very moment. But since when did love make sense? Standing up here, or driving those windy roads, or watching an approaching train, we gamble. We feel the power granted us at that moment, and our intellect and our emotions and our instincts all have their say. And the amazing, beautiful, possibly transcendent thing about humanity is that we almost always bet on ourselves."

* * *

When they first opened Ericsson Stadium in Charlotte, North Carolina, it was touted as one of the most high-tech stadiums ever made. They hired a man to stand on the roof and point a satellite dish at a blimp to get out the television feed.

—Jason

MY RELATIONSHIP VENN DIAGRAM

CONTINUING THE THREAD OF our typical reader, this is probably the most common sentiment we see from our submitters. Not just love-related, this is the most common sentiment, period. I'm going out on a limb a bit here, but it seems like dating can be pretty hard and even a bit depressing. Certainly, it is the subject people most like to complain about. However, whenever people start getting too down on dating I always remind them, it could be worse; you could be Horace.

We are a culture obsessed with dating, and it has us going a little crazy. It actually worries me how many depressing dating charts we see. Everybody seems to be frustrated and manic and bitter. So much so that it seems like people actually hate to see each other happy at times.

Now I'm no expert on how to do this the right way. If I was, I wouldn't be single (a mildly agoraphobic, neurotic,

cyborg, happy-factory who obsesses about jumping from high places...and single?! I know, crazy). However, I think it's time we got a bit of an attitude adjustment about our love lives. Yes, that's right, we are going to solve the problems with love in a book about charts—buckle up.

The problem is that most of us have a surprisingly unnuanced (for how much time we spend obsessing on the topic) view of love and relationships. Everything is all or nothing, perfect or horrible, true love or wasted time. This binary view of love makes us lock people and emotions into bizarre, static, *Cosmo*-cover relationships. We end up thinking everything is simple and easily manipulable and predictable. You did this, it must mean this! I feel this, it must mean this!

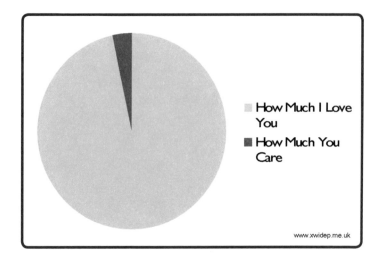

How Much I Love You

How Much You Care

www.xwidep.me.uk

This mind-set never gives people the room to be people. So it shouldn't, then, be a surprise when we have trouble loving somebody we have not allowed to be a person, since ostensibly we are looking for a person to fall in love with. We cut off the very thing we are looking for: unpredictability.

People are constantly evolving and learning, and their needs are constantly changing. We look different each day, but each day also courts a different part of our personality. The choices of others are not as prescriptive as most would have you believe. For some reason, this terrifies most people and they don't want to deal with it. We think of change in broad, shallow terms. We want our partners to change, but we want to be in charge. We do disgusting things like "train" them to be who we want them to be.

Love is not a single thing, won and held onto. It is a combination of emotions put under one roof, between people who are a combination of their different selves put under one roof. And these people and this love are expected to exist over time without alteration? That sounds incredibly dumb to me. I barely have any idea who I am, all the chapters of this book about agency aside, so why should I expect my significant other to be static? Actually, that is the last thing I would want. Because we fear changes in our surroundings, and often in ourselves, we try to freeze the world around us, and just like most bad habits, the impact of this is felt mostly by the ones we love.

This is one of my favorite series of charts because it tells a clear story and because it shows the complexity of a relationship.

DATING

SUMMER LOVE

I Love Charts

EVERYTHING TOGETHER

TRACKS

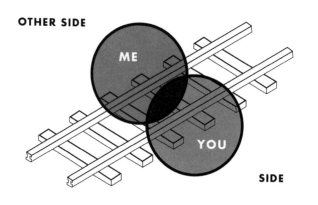

OTHER SIDE

ME

YOU

SIDE

LONG DISTANCE

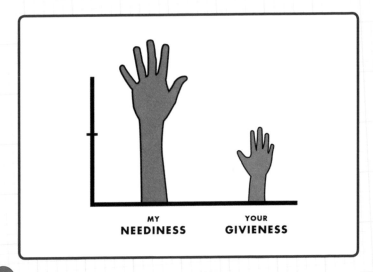

MY
NEEDINESS

YOUR
GIVIENESS

**TOO GOOD
TO BE TRUE**

BREAKUP

We need to accept complexity and allow for ourselves and those around us to change. We obsess over love, but usually focus on flat stories and how-to guides. Our relationships reflect those choices. In stories, characters have the limitation of space and their designed purpose. Those limitations are comforting. With people, there are no such limitations. There is no purpose, and every moment is part of the story. When you are with somebody, they are not offering you a character, but a whole universe equal in scale to your own, and it is pretty incredible that anybody would want to share that with you.

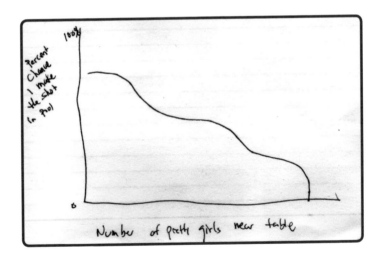

Enjoy the process, from the depressing parts, to the silly parts, to the comfortable parts. But mostly enjoy that it can and will change and that means you are doing something right.

Just don't get too comfortable...

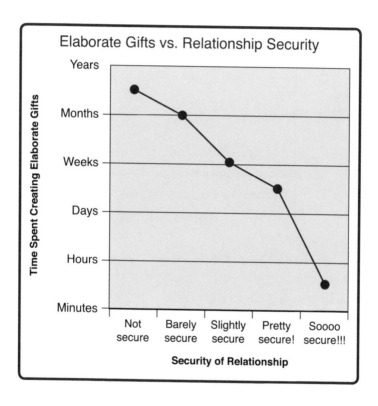

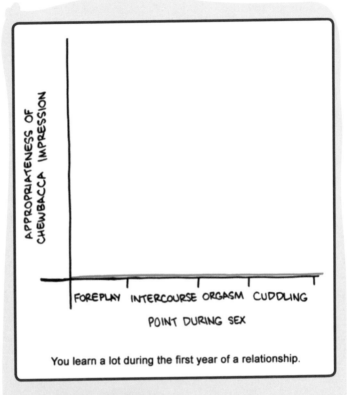

You learn a lot during the first year of a relationship.

CODY'S QUIP

WHILE WE'RE ON THE TOPIC: HAIR DOLLS. It turns out hair dolls are another thing to never mention during sex. Don't ask.

CATS

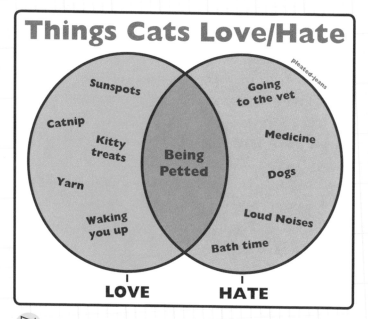

Things Cats Love/Hate

pleated-jeans

Sunspots

Catnip

Kitty treats

Yarn

Waking you up

Being Petted

Going to the vet

Medicine

Dogs

Loud Noises

Bath time

LOVE **HATE**

Cats are safe to make fun of. No one is going to call me out for making fun of cats. If I go after dogs, forget it, the angry emails will start rolling in, but cats are fair game. Nobody stands up for the bully when the downtrodden extract their verbal vengeance. That dude totally had it coming. And no one is going to stand up for cats because they are total jerks.

Dogs trade loyalty for comfort; cats trade tolerance. I can't make fun of dogs because we have an even relationship with them—they do things to help the people who shelter and feed them. A dog will protect you and play with you and greet you eagerly when you come home. Plus dogs are dumb.

Dogs always have this doofy expression on their faces, and as humans, we just love that about them. It's right in our wheelhouse. We love loyalty but don't really trust anything that is smart enough to machinate against us. Dogs are perfect; they'll protect us from intruders, but sometimes they'll also eat clearly inedible things off the counter. We feel safe because there is no threat of conspiracy.

We admire dogs for their simple loyalty. We give them food and they give us love and the newspaper. Somewhere in our hearts we all know that if we were more like dogs, the world would be a better place.

But instead, we are more like cats, and the world kind of sucks.

Cats are the teenagers of the animal kingdom. They want what they want and if you disagree, they hate you and hide up in their rooms. They'll wake you up in the middle of the night because they are hungry, but they'll look at you like *you're* the one with the problem when you make them get up and move so you can make the bed at noon. Cats stay out all night and come home the next day with unexplained wounds. Cats will meow and cry for food and then look at you with disdain when it's not the right kind. Cats sit around with their friends in the basement doing catnip and listening to Pink Floyd while you sit upstairs like you don't know what they're doing down there. Cats are jerks.

And cats are too smart to be trusted. They sit aloof, watching, removed from any situation. Cats seem completely capable of conspiracy. They are vindictive. I have proof.

My parents have a cat that seeks out my stuff whenever possible and urinates on it. No one else's stuff, just mine. And this has been going on for *years*. The cat schemes and plots and waits for the opportunity to strike, and when she strikes, she strikes deliberately and without remorse. There is a cold complacency in her actions.

All through high school I couldn't leave the door to my bedroom open. If I stepped away for even a moment, I would return to find golden revenge exacted on my carpet. All because I stood *near* the dog and didn't prevent her from bounding after the cat. Years of closed doors for being an amused though innocent bystander.

Maybe that isn't completely true. Maybe I *slightly* encouraged the dog to chase her. Whatever, it's irrelevant. The punishment still doesn't fit the crime.

Having a cat that pees on your stuff and in your room may not seem like a big deal, but you weren't there man, you don't know what it was like. I would be in the bathroom and in a moment of uncertain panic, wonder if my door was open. I would leave the house, walk to my car, turn around, and run back inside just to make sure I had closed my door. It got to the point where that cat didn't even need to get into my bedroom, she was already in my head. There was never a moment of rest, never a moment of respite. I spent years living with the constant anxiety of returning to a urine-soaked bed, which let me tell you, is a very specific and unpleasant type of anxiety.

I apologized. I put down food for her whenever she was hungry. I tried to block the dog from running after her. But neither did she forgive nor forget. She stayed constantly vigilant, day in and day out, year in and year out. With the setting of the sun, the turning of the seasons, the twisting of the heavens, she remained, eyes trained on the room where I laid my head to sleep. Waiting. Waiting to take her revenge again and again. Waiting to defile my sanctum as I had once defiled her tranquility. One gets the feeling that if she had opposable thumbs, I would have awoken many mornings to find decapitated voodoo dolls nailed to my door.

And you know what? She won. She broke me. In the summer, the closed door meant my room had no cross breeze and was sweltering in the afternoon sun. Every time I entered, I was afraid I'd find more of my stuff soaking with revenge. Every time I was away, I was terrified of coming home to a door left open. Like a torture victim, I crawled back to her, drenched in sweat, half mad, unable to see through the waking nightmare my life had become. I pleaded for a truce. I begged. On my

I Love Charts

hands and knees, with my face pressed firmly to the floor, I cried, "Please, no more!" And there she stood, master of my sanity. Did she show compassion? Did she show mercy? Was there a hint of forgiveness? No. She went and peed on my stuff that was sitting in the hallway.

I've met the eyes of a cat, looked deep into its soul, and I have come away a husk of the man I was. Seriously, cats are jerks.

And so I feel at ease knocking cats down a few pegs. They need it. But like the bad boy with the heart of gold, we still love them. They may torture us and torment us, but we love them. Maybe it's Stockholm syndrome. Maybe cats have psychologically abused us more than we even realize. But every once in a while, when it's late at night and everyone else is asleep, you hear a creak on the stairs. And through the door and into the living room creeps your tormentor. You tense up, but in the soft glow of the television you see that her eyes hold something different and you are no longer afraid. She lulls you to sleep with her rhythmic purring and soft fur and you drift away peacefully.

When you awake, you find that the cat has gone, but your lap is warm, and you smile. You walk upstairs to bed thinking that maybe cats aren't really that mean after all. And then, comfortable in a way you haven't been in years, you sit on the edge of your bed and think one final thought before you lie back to sleep: "Wait, why is my sock wet?"

—Cody

I Love Charts

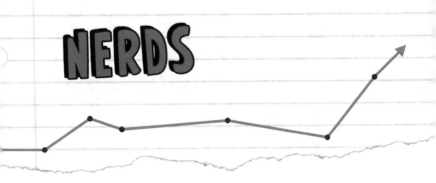

NERDS

THIS BOOK WOULD NOT be complete without a love letter of sorts to nerds, so that's why we set aside an entire chapter for them. Without nerds, we would not be writing this book. My love goes deeper than that though; nerds are my favorite people on earth. Here's why: nerds care. They care alot.

Now, if you live with a nerd who is reading this book, there is a 75 percent chance you are now reading this passage because the nerd in question threw this book away (possibly at you) in disgust a few moments ago. If that is the case, please find the nerd in question, return this book, and assure them that (1) they need not be disgusted, and (2) they have passed the nerd test. Then further explain to them that, in the sentence immediately preceding this paragraph, I was addressing an imaginary creature that resembles a cross between a bear, a yak,

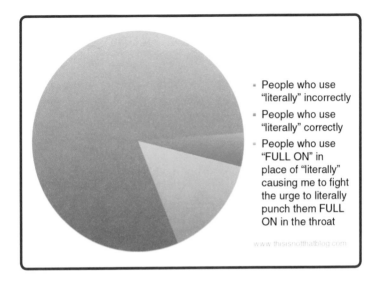

- People who use "literally" incorrectly
- People who use "literally" correctly
- People who use "FULL ON" in place of "literally" causing me to fight the urge to literally punch them FULL ON in the throat

www.thisisnotthatblog.com

and a pug, not ruining their precious English language (shout out, Allie Brosh).

Welcome back, nerds. Sorry to have infuriated you; I was just trying to make a point. Nerds care a lot.

For those of you who are not nerds and are lost right now, please contact a nerd with whom you are friendly and read them the previous page. They will either get the reference and be able to talk you through it, or will Google enough things to be able to explain it to you momentarily. I'm letting you off the hook for Google duty since you are currently holding this book, which my publisher assures me does not have Internet access. (The previous sentence will not be omitted from electronic versions of this book, to further irritate nerds.)

So what exactly do nerds care so much about? While there is certainly no one rule that in the darkness binds them, the commonality is that nerds have a commitment to learning. They also have a fairly meritocratic view on subject matter. If there is something of value to be learned, there are nerds who are committed to learning it, regardless (and often in spite) of how uninteresting it appears at face value. And that is ultimately why I love nerds. They know awesome things.

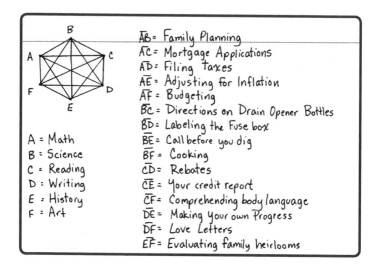

$\overline{AB}$ = Family Planning
$\overline{AC}$ = Mortgage Applications
$\overline{AD}$ = Filing Taxes
$\overline{AE}$ = Adjusting for Inflation
$\overline{AF}$ = Budgeting
$\overline{BC}$ = Directions on Drain Opener Bottles
$\overline{BD}$ = Labeling the Fuse box
$\overline{BE}$ = Call before you dig
$\overline{BF}$ = Cooking
$\overline{CD}$ = Rebates
$\overline{CE}$ = Your credit report
$\overline{CF}$ = Comprehending body language
$\overline{DE}$ = Making your own Progress
$\overline{DF}$ = Love Letters
$\overline{EF}$ = Evaluating family heirlooms

A = Math
B = Science
C = Reading
D = Writing
E = History
F = Art

It is not just me, there is a lot of the nerd love going around. There has never been a better time to be a nerd. We live in an increasingly meritocratic culture, so those

The Six Stages of Movie Geek Evolution

Familymovius cartoonata

Movie Geek Evolution begins at the most basic level. Familymovius cartoonata forages for visual stimulation with clear cut messages of right and wrong, good and evil. He/she is indoctrinated with "life lessons," and is prone to watching a favorite film over and over and over again. Princes and princesses are abundant.

FAVORITE MOVIES: *Snow White; Cars; The Lion King*

Blockbustericus

Evolution rolls on with simple, slightly more adult themes. In the male of the species, explosions and comedy are emphasized. In the female, the emphasis is placed on romance and socialization. Superhero movies often satisfy both cravings. More evolved members of the species may use films as part of the early mating ritual, contingent upon avoiding their nemesis—chaperones.

FAVORITE MOVIES: *Twilight; Spider-Man*

Sundancicus robustus

While still not fully understanding how to use the tools of film geekery, Sundancicus has a powerful thirst for knowledge. Having tired of love stories and things blowing up, he/she seeks out the next level of evolution—independent cinema. The peak of Sundancicus' evolution occurs after tackling lots and lots of movies about heroin and seeking to impress more evolved mating partners.

FAVORITE MOVIES: *Trainspotting; Reservoir Dogs; Requiem for a Dream*

I Love Charts

Oscaria subtitlus

Eventually, independent films and heroin grow tiresome. This prompts evolution. Oscaria begins to seek out award winning films. He/she no longer refers to subtitled films as "reading." There is an awareness that lots of incredible movies were created in years other than the recently completed decade. He/she becomes aware of nuances like cinematography, dialogue, and character foils.

FAVORITE MOVIES: *Citizen Kane; Rashomon; Requiem for a Dream*

Filmsnobicus hipsterata

Many may consider this an evolutionary step backwards. However, it's a necessary evil. Filmsnobicus has learned a great deal about movies, but expresses these lessons in the most aggressive and annoying way possible. Filmsnobicus is liable to refer to foreign films only by their foreign title. An "irony" mutation often develops. Needing a break from classics and subtitled films, yet still seeking to enhance their knowledge, Filmsnobicus may turn to Troma or exploitation.

FAVORITE MOVIES: *Aguirre, der Zorn Gottes; Transmorphers*

Celluloid sapien

The evolutionary step from Filmsnobicus to Celluloid Sapien occurs upon realizing the error of aggressive ways. Motivations shift away from snark, and towards finding ways to share the love of cinema. This includes learning about the deepest nuances of filmmaking. Celluloid Sapien is generous with even the most obscure titles in his/her collection because it results in the acquisition of the greatest desire: enhanced film discussion. Most importantly, he/she accepts a world in which all films of all qualities and genres can co-exist amongst their respective audiences.

FAVORITE MOVIES: Whatever they're watching at the time

who have committed themselves to acquiring knowledge and skills are at an advantage even more so than usual. Professional athletes are dressing like nerds. Unfunny, unrealistic, misguided, pandering TV shows and movies are being made about nerds. Computer and Internet literacy (typically strong suits for nerds) are nearly mandatory. But most importantly, it is just plain cool to be smart and to have esoteric interests. And yes, hipsters are partially to thank for that, just like they are to thank for reinvigorating a culture of meritocracy. Deal with it.

Hipsters and nerds actually share a lot of common ground, though there is a huge disparity in self-identification. You would be hard-pressed to find somebody who cops to being a hipster, but everybody these days wants to call themselves a nerd. Culture's rush to embrace the nerd has been confusing for those of us who actually are nerds (and to be fair, I can only barely call myself a nerd; I have gazed into the depths of nerddom and am far from worthy). Most true nerds are born of isolation more than of acceptance, and so the idea of acceptance, let alone cultural cachet, sits rather oddly.

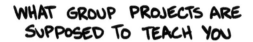

WHAT GROUP PROJECTS ARE SUPPOSED TO TEACH YOU

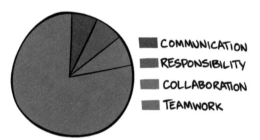

COMMUNICATION
RESPONSIBILITY
COLLABORATION
TEAMWORK

WHAT GROUP PROJECTS TAUGHT ME

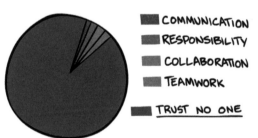

COMMUNICATION
RESPONSIBILITY
COLLABORATION
TEAMWORK

TRUST NO ONE

endlessorigami.com

CODY'S QUIP

OR THE MOST IMPORTANT LESSON OF ALL: If you sit back and let other people argue, you can get away with doing almost no work at all.

You see, the strength of the nerd comes from isolation and alienation overcome. The journey builds character, gives perspective, and other clichés I can't think of right now. One does not simply walk into nerddom. There is always the origin story.

Our hero is born into isolation, shunned by the normative world. Though young, it is clear that the nerd is different, has something special, indefinable, awkward. Without the distracting lure of socializing, the nerd turns to the intense pursuit of very specific interests. Our budding nerd learns to love a subject, a genre, any piece of intellectual property to call his or her home. Doggedly, the nerd pursues the subject, delving deeper into the obscure, the precise, the esoteric beyond any possible relevance.

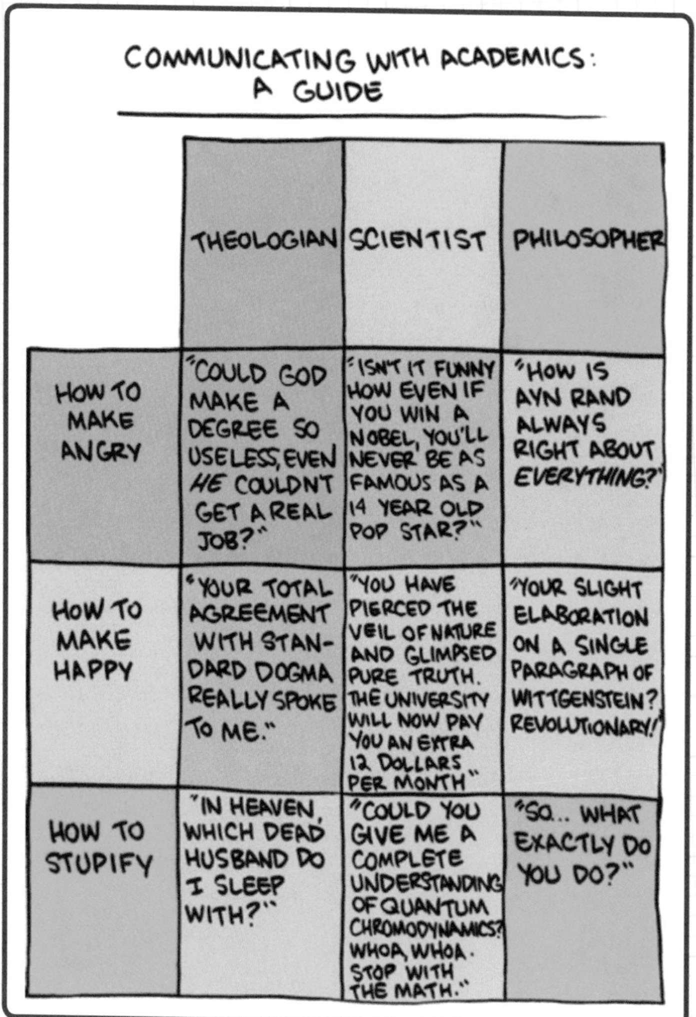

COMMUNICATING WITH ACADEMICS: A GUIDE

	THEOLOGIAN	SCIENTIST	PHILOSOPHER
HOW TO MAKE ANGRY	"COULD GOD MAKE A DEGREE SO USELESS, EVEN HE COULDN'T GET A REAL JOB?"	"ISN'T IT FUNNY HOW EVEN IF YOU WIN A NOBEL, YOU'LL NEVER BE AS FAMOUS AS A 14 YEAR OLD POP STAR?"	"HOW IS AYN RAND ALWAYS RIGHT ABOUT EVERYTHING?"
HOW TO MAKE HAPPY	"YOUR TOTAL AGREEMENT WITH STANDARD DOGMA REALLY SPOKE TO ME."	"YOU HAVE PIERCED THE VEIL OF NATURE AND GLIMPSED PURE TRUTH. THE UNIVERSITY WILL NOW PAY YOU AN EXTRA 12 DOLLARS PER MONTH"	"YOUR SLIGHT ELABORATION ON A SINGLE PARAGRAPH OF WITTGENSTEIN? REVOLUTIONARY!"
HOW TO STUPIFY	"IN HEAVEN, WHICH DEAD HUSBAND DO I SLEEP WITH?"	"COULD YOU GIVE ME A COMPLETE UNDERSTANDING OF QUANTUM CHROMODYNAMICS? WHOA, WHOA. STOP WITH THE MATH."	"SO... WHAT EXACTLY DO YOU DO?"

NeRds 69

And then one fine morning, in one fine basement or message board or classroom, the nerd discovers that there are others. There are more out there with the special powers of observation and obsession honed from years of ostracism. Communities form around interests, combine expertise, create their own languages. The nerd grows strong.

It is at this point that something beautiful happens. Given enough time to explore a subject, the nerd makes a true leap of genius. Let us pause here, for "leap" is not a word chosen lightly. I believe that genius is best described as the ability to wield abstract thought with great dimensions. Let's say an idea consists of the connection of point A to point B. The closer those points usually are to each other, the easier your job is. Example: it is pretty simple to understand that cars mean freedom. You are more flexible with a car than with most other modes of transportation, which offers you freedom. That cars represent America takes a little bit more work. Cars are freedom. America models itself as freedom incarnate. Cars to freedom to America. We have added a step. That the American obsession with cars has something to do with its historical emphasis on the imagery of freedom and individuality and also with the sentimentality with which America views itself, given a history of self-reverence, is yet another step. And so on. A genius does two things: (1) loads point B into a T-shirt cannon and launches it farther away from point A than anybody had thought possible, and (2) finds a way to communicate the journey between the two points in a way that the rest of us can follow. Step one is the leap of genius, step two is the hard work.

Anyway, back to our nerd. The leap of genius a nerd makes is the same that many great artists make. Having ventured far afield in a painfully specific area of thought, having sacrificed time and other pleasures (often sanity, or at least the ability to socialize), the nerd/artist stands at point B and realizes its worth, realizes that somewhere in that humble hamlet in which all great heroes are born lies point A, and decides to connect the two. The nerd figures out a way to connect all that hard-earned knowledge back to the normative culture from which he or she once fled. Something intellectual and abstract is made human and given context within the human condition.

And so the nerd returns triumphant to society, exclaiming, "For humanity, I have devoted my life to the noble pursuit of this one true idea! I'm really into *Battlestar Galactica* and this is why it is important!" And nobody listens.

The end.

The problem, of course, is language. Most nerds, again like most great artists, need a translator to help communicate the relevance of their ideas and interests with the world. Luckily, charts have proven to be a reliable medium for showing the value of nerdy expertise. They are useful in telling those stories that so need to be told, the tales of our adventuring nerds.

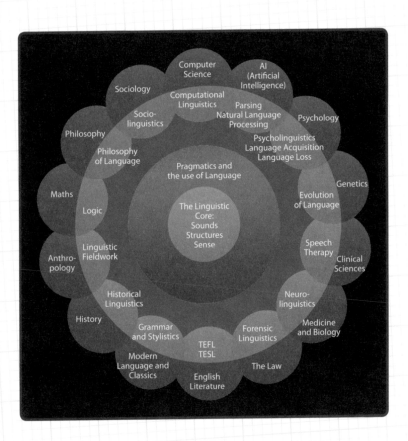

I Love Charts

It also helps that nerds, again like hipsters (how's that for a genius leap? I'm stringing a line through nerds, hipsters, and great artists—nailed it), can lead you to some cultural gems that are well worth exploration. Nerds and hipsters liked this stuff before the rest of us could even recognize its potential merit; it's okay to admit it. So, dear readers, embrace the nerd like I have. Revel in their discoveries, thank them for their hard work, help them communicate their passion, and know that when you are with a nerd, you are in the presence of a hero.

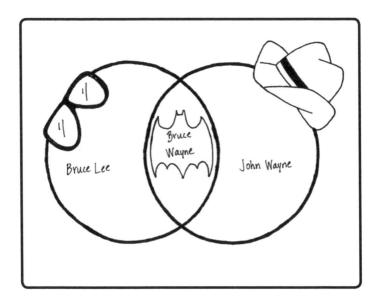

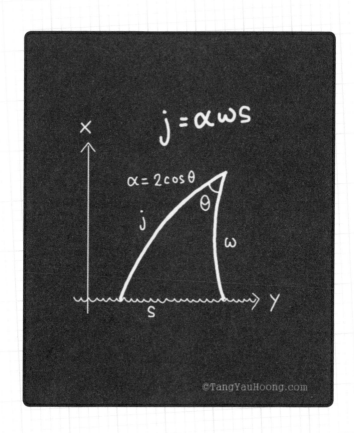

I Love Charts

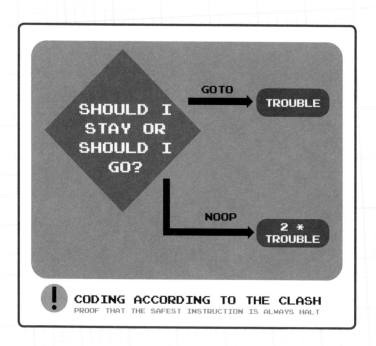

CODING ACCORDING TO THE CLASH
PROOF THAT THE SAFEST INSTRUCTION IS ALWAYS HALT

Primer
a comprehensive timeline

by Laura Ells

▸ ● & ● are working on an invention, a device that will partially block gravity, making objects lighter.

▸ ● discovers that they unknowingly made a time machine and builds two versions big enough for humans: ■ and □, intent to keep □ a secret in case the need to reset everything arises.

Sunday

▸ ● calls in sick to work and isolates himself in a hotel room.

▸ ● enters ■ and gets out after 6 hours.

▸ ● meets up with ●, and tells him about the device, showing him ● enter the storage facility where ■ and □ are being kept.

▸ ● & ● make ■.

▸ At a party ● is threatened by ● with a shot-gun. ● & ● are not at the party but hear about the event.

Monday

▸ ● drugs ● and hides him in the attic.

▸ ● meets up with ● and tells him about the device, showing him ● enter the storage facility where ■ & □ are being kept. ● is recording all of his conversations.

▸ ● goes to the party and stops ● but fails to send him to jail, leaving ● still in potential danger.

▸ ● uses □ again, creating ●.

Monday

▸ ● waits for ● to drug ● and then attacks ● but loses because he is exhausted from time traveling. However, ● convinces ● to leave.

▸ ● meets up with ● and tells him about the device, showing him ● enter the storage facility where ■ & □ are being kept. ● uses the recordings ● made to help him.

▸ ● goes to the party and stops ●, making sure this time that ● will be arrested, saving ● and becoming a hero.

Monday

▸ ● gasses ● and hides hm in the closet.

▸ ● meets ●, intending to not tell him about the device, but ● collapses from exhaustion due to time travel.

▸ ● tells ● about □ and that his is not ●.

▸ ● reluctantly goes to the party with ● and helps him engineer the events, sending ● to jail once again, protecting ●.

Monday

I Love Charts

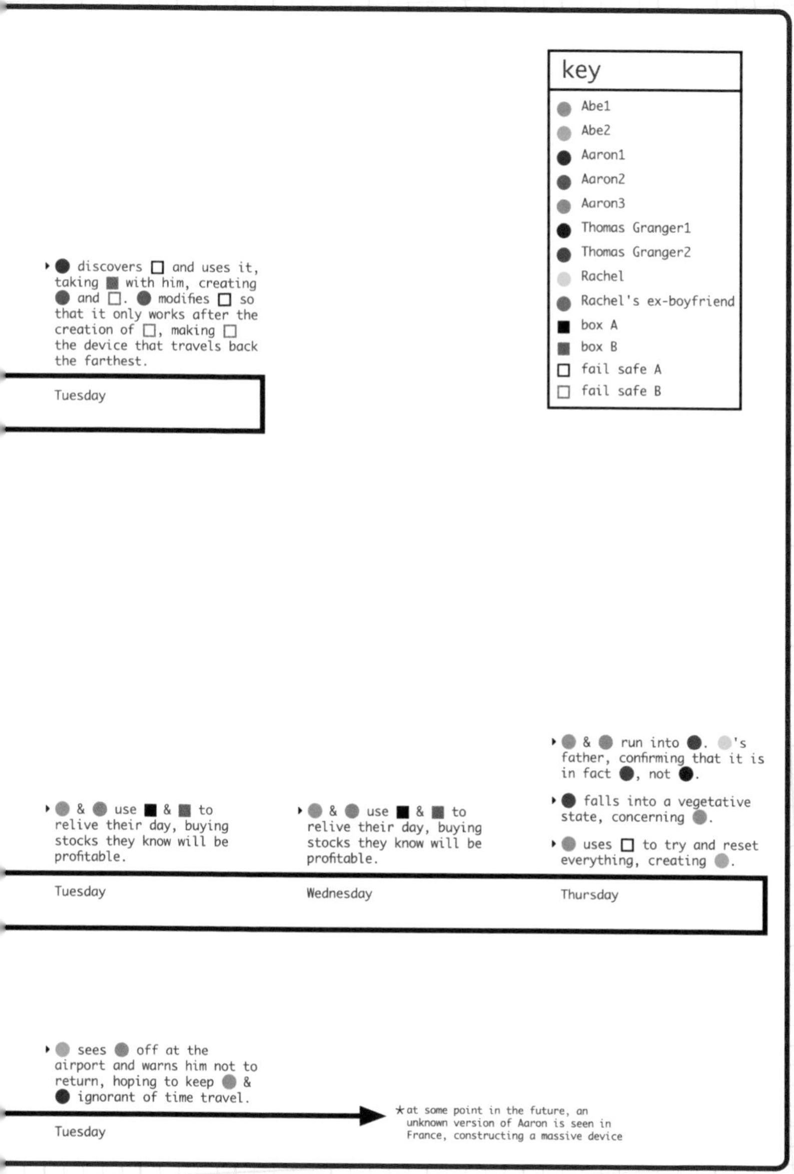

key
● Abe1
● Abe2
● Aaron1
● Aaron2
● Aaron3
● Thomas Granger1
● Thomas Granger2
● Rachel
● Rachel's ex-boyfriend
■ box A
■ box B
□ fail safe A
□ fail safe B

▸ ● discovers □ and uses it, taking ■ with him, creating ● and □. ● modifies □ so that it only works after the creation of □, making □ the device that travels back the farthest.

Tuesday

▸ ● & ● use ■ & ■ to relive their day, buying stocks they know will be profitable.

Tuesday

▸ ● & ● use ■ & ■ to relive their day, buying stocks they know will be profitable.

Wednesday

▸ ● & ● run into ●. ●'s father, confirming that it is in fact ●, not ●.

▸ ● falls into a vegetative state, concerning ●.

▸ ● uses □ to try and reset everything, creating ●.

Thursday

▸ ● sees ● off at the airport and warns him not to return, hoping to keep ● & ● ignorant of time travel.

Tuesday

★ at some point in the future, an unknown version of Aaron is seen in France, constructing a massive device

Nerds 77

MAGIC

⬦ One time, I was playing Dungeons and Dragons while mild-ly intoxicated and came up with a great idea. Not just a great idea, my best idea. Before I share the idea, you need to know two things. First, you need to know that everybody I was playing with thought the idea was dumb. Second, you need to know that everybody I was playing with is an idiot, with horrible taste.

I'm kidding of course. A D&D game is built on a foundation of trust, mutual respect, Thai food, and ice-cold Bud Lights. I would never accuse those who choose to venture forth with me of having anything less than the finest intellectual credentials. That said, those guys are jerks. Straight up cat-level jerks.

My idea, which was so hastily and prematurely put down, involves upgrading the standard magic system by...whoa! Hang in there, not-nerds. Don't go anywhere. This will be interesting for you too, I promise. It is, after all, a great idea. Anyway, it involves visualizing magic in relation to strict reality, using a bit of simple Newtonian physics, with a dash of science from my kindred mustache, Paul Dirac. Top with some linguistic tomfoolery and you have my crowning achievement: subnatural magic.

Picture a pendulum at rest, hanging perpendicular to the floor. Let's call that position "reality." Pull the pendulum to the left (see, even Galileo is in on my great idea). The farther from the equilibrium position the pendulum is pulled, the farther from "reality" it is. Let's then call everything to the left of center "super-reality." Wait, I think we can do better than that. Everything that happens in "reality" is natural. It is comprised of only natural occurrences, strict science, nothing wacky. That means that everything left of center is "supernatural," which is actually a real word. Much better.

So now we have our pendulum pulled to the left of center, and since that area is now supernatural, it is fair to say that the farther we pull it from the center, the more supernatural things become. Close to the equilibrium position, not much is out of the ordinary. Far away, things barely resemble the natural world we live in.

Let's then apply this model to a person, say a mage. The pendulum is now a scale for how supernatural that person can be, or more simply, how much magical ability they have. After all, magic is basically anything that exceeds natural laws. Fire in the fireplace is normal: reality. Fire in somebody's hand makes no sense: magic. However, you can still picture fire in somebody's hand; the deviation from reality is not overwhelming, so the pendulum is only pulled over a bit. Fire shooting out of the clouds in columns: really strong magic. Pull the pendulum way to the left.

Now, release the pendulum and what does it do? It swings back down, through the equilibrium position and way up to the right. As it is falling from the left to center, it is increasing the natural and decreasing the supernatural. As it passes through center and goes to the right, it is once again moving from the natural, though in a different direction, so it can no longer be called "supernatural"; it should be called "subnatural." There you have it. Subnatural, the opposite of supernatural. If supernatural is magic, then subnatural is antimagic, the negative to the print of the magic world.

So, what does that mean?

Well, unless we are talking about spectroscopic lines or quantum mechanics (and thankfully, we are not), it means that subnatural magic does the opposite of what magic does. If magic makes things unreal, antimagic should make things extra-real.

And what is more real than science? Subnatural magic should be science-based. If you are a powerful subnatural mage, you should be able to actually understand spectroscopic lines and quantum mechanics, and use them in battle. You should be able to use electricity. You should get a gun. To be clear, we are starting from a standard fantasy D&D game here—swords, arrows, mail, elves, dwarves, halflings, etc., so a gun would be quite a handy advancement.

The technology has to be tied to the subnatural mage, otherwise you dilute the value of his or her expertise and alter the gaming universe too much, so make it such that each bit of technology has a required subnatural skill level to use. If your grunt soldier picks up the gun, it will do nothing for him. Think of the subnatural mage as a conjurer who conjures tools for him or herself. Bionic leg? Rifle? Car? Just level up enough. All the wonders of science at your fingertips.

Here is the final, most ridiculed wrinkle to my idea, one last bit of linguistic fun. How does one increase subnatural ability? How does one get extra-real? By simply keeping it real. In my proposed D&D universe, keeping it real is as much a lifestyle obsession as it is in our universe, only with more to gain. If you do something deemed by your Dungeon Master (the arbiter of all **D&D** adventures) as keeping it real, you gain experience. Not through kills, or missions, just by living the life and keeping it real. Refuse to go on a mission because you don't want to harm any goblins? If that's you, do you. Level up. Eschew wearing armor because it looks bulky? Keeping it real. Level up. Tell your party leader he is being an idiot? Real talk. Level up. Have to split from a battle to feed the kids? Grown-man action there. Level up. Character too hungover to fight? That's life. Level up.

How much better does this make Dungeons and Dragons?! You get random technology when you want it and you open up a whole new character action reward system! Genius, I know. So, keep it real with me (by the way, sorry non-nerds, I lied; this is just about D&D). Subnatural magic: great idea or the greatest idea?

—Jason

I Love Charts

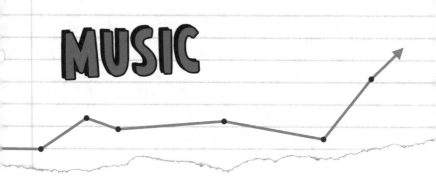

MUSIC

I BROUGHT UP HIPSTERS earlier and now seems like a perfect time to bring that beat back. When you talk about hipsters (and yes, tired though the subject may be and a half-decade removed from their heyday, people do still talk about them), the conversation inevitably becomes about taste. Well, isn't taste just a form of curation? If you look at hipsters as cultural anthropologists, it's no surprise that the rise of hipster culture to mainstream visibility came in the same period as the rise of the nerd, meritocracy, populism, and the blogger-as-professional-curator. The connecting material here is an emphasis on the aesthetic quality of the work rather than its mass appeal, and an interest in the individual connected with the work rather than the institution. More simply put, it is narrowing the focus down to the work or the individual while trying to weed out whatever else muddies the picture.

I Love Charts

Successful curation means learning from the nerds and the artists and finding ways to expand on a central idea, while always being able to make leaps back to the human element, the reason for the exploration. Obscurity for obscurity's sake is never a good idea. Remember, the distance of point B from point A only matters if you can connect the two. If you can't, you do not have ownership of the idea and you are essentially bluffing.

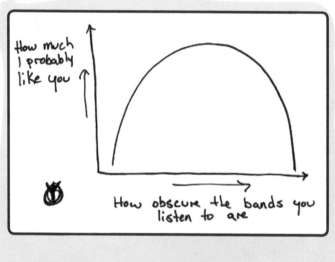

CODY'S QUIP

Also known as the NPR bubble.

I have two tips for aspiring curators. First, know your own limits. People usually know when you are bluffing, so stay within what you know, and if you want to add to your repertoire, do your research first and then add. Your job is to research everything you curate and to be able to stand by what you write, even when that means discovering that what you wrote is wrong. And you should be wrong; it is helpful. You should always be learning and adapting and tweaking the formulae.

Second, understand that your personality can help you, but it shouldn't dominate your work. Just because something is interesting to you doesn't mean that it will be of interest to other people (obviously), but beyond that it doesn't even mean it's a fully formed idea. If you are truly interested in something, take the time to study enough to have something to present to people further than "I am interested in this." The connection part of the genius leap is the hard work, but once again, that is your job. It's hard being a genius, isn't it?

So now, in my capacity as curator, here are some of our favorite music-related charts.

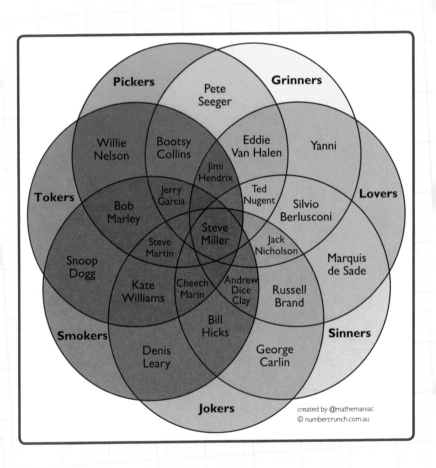

created by @mathemaniac
© numbercrunch.com.au

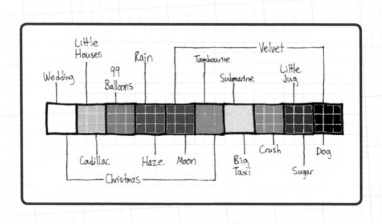

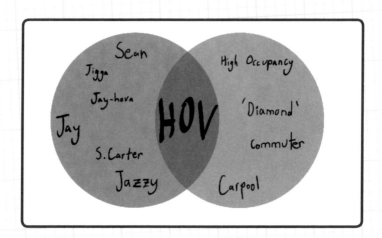

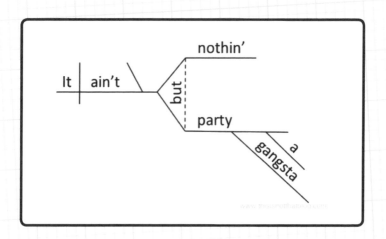

I Love Charts

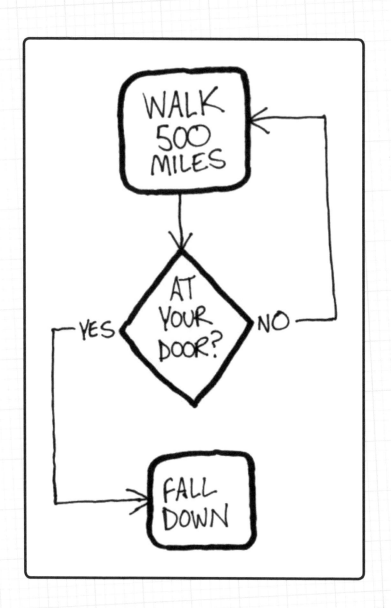

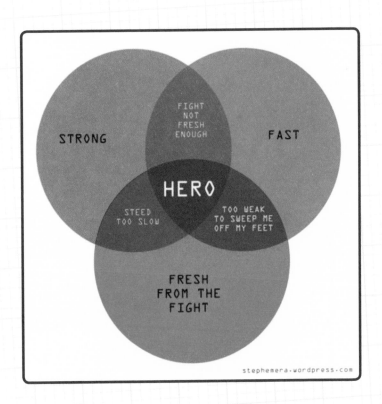

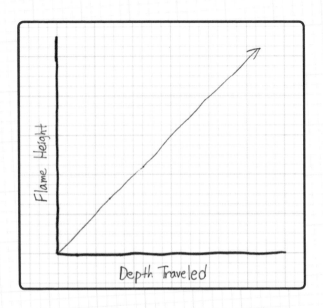

DESTINATION	HOW TO GET THERE
Nowhere	Road
Anywhere	Midnight Train
Georgia	Midnight Train
Clarksville	Last Train
Heaven	Stairway
Hell	Highway
Hotel California	Dark Desert Highway

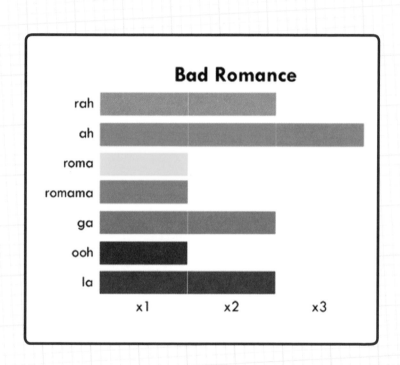

I Love Charts

And finally, while we are on Gaga, here's an interesting bit of information.

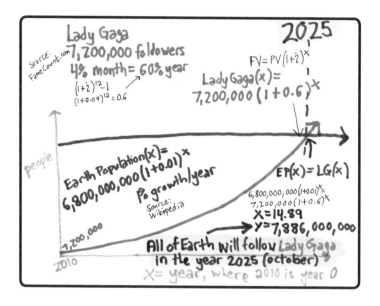

Lady Gaga
Source: FameCount.com
7,200,000 followers
4% month = 60% year
$\frac{(1+2)^{12}-1}{(1+0.04)^{12}} = 0.6$

2025

$FV = PV(1+2)^x$
Lady Gaga$(x) = $
$7,200,000(1+0.6)^x$

Earth Population$(x) = $
$6,800,000,000(1+0.01)^x$
1% growth/year
Source: Wikipedia

people

1,200,000

2010

$EP(x) = LG(x)$
$6,800,000,000(1+0.01)^x = $
$7,200,000(1+0.6)^x$
$X = 14.89$
$Y = 7,886,000,000$

All of Earth will follow Lady Gaga in the year 2025 (october)
$X = $ year, where 2010 is year 0

CHANCE

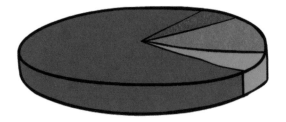

SKILLS OF A TOUR GUIDE

- PUBLIC SPEAKING
- KNOWING LOTS OF FUN FACTS
- ENTERTAINING
- BEING ABLE TO WALK BACKWARDS WITHOUT EATING SHIT

endlessorigami.com

Freshman year. Picture it. It's early afternoon, class started twenty minutes ago, and I'm sitting on my dorm room floor playing PlayStation, trying to negotiate the trade deadline and guide the Milwaukee Brewers to a pennant. My friends are all sitting around, trying to negotiate final paper deadlines and guide Milwaukee Bests to their mouths.

We're all in need of a good pitcher. The windows, blinds half drawn, cast shadows across the bemired carpet. Life lesson: beige is a color for the steady-handed and sober, or those with the resolve to clean a carpet now and then. Ah, freshman year. Do not weep! Tomorrow is a Good Friday. Come Sunday, roll back the keystone and see what you find. Or rather, if it is more your speed, roll back the key stoned. No matter, those tests don't come until after graduation.

Religious studies, philosophy, biology, chemistry: subjects I studied but never took classes in. Books as props for beer pong tables and Parents' Weekend—education through libation. Sociology: Intro to Adult Group Dynamics. History: One Hundred and One Uses for a Trojan Horse. A course, of course, occasionally, but let's be honest, the academic portion of my education wasn't to begin in earnest for at least another three semesters.

Academia, the destination, was just a point on a map and we'd been lost since orientation.

In short, we were drunk on knowledge, shorter still we were just drunk. The Truth was like the booze, proof secondary to acquisition and quantity. And it flowed freely. Like Greeks, we gathered in robes and thongs to debate the world.

Methodically Socratic, we were culturally hedonistic. The dorm room was our crowded acropolis, replete with iconic columns of recycling—empty cases and pages. We bore the burden of enlightenment, and though we waxed invective, we knew it all and shared freely and without solicitation.

Though we diligently pursued the intoxicating elixir of truth, our attentions were occasionally diverted by beer runs and the, albeit infrequent, obligatory guilt-fueled trip to class.

Sometimes streakers would suspend our sophistry. Dance parties demanded participation. Once, I remember, we slept. And sometimes, on a clear crisp sunny afternoon, a tour of prospective students would pass by the dorm.

Oh, prospective students. We all remember being one. The aggressively enthusiastic and suspiciously friendly student guides. The thinly veiled questions. What's the social life like here (are the parties good)? Are the people nice (will the people sleep with me)? You're going to be a senior next year (will *you* sleep with me)? Seeing those confused kids made us nostalgic for the old, innocent days…five months ago. But you can't ungrow or unlearn, so as mature, educated adults, we would observe, reminisce, and occasionally interfere.

Whenever someone would see a tour approaching, we would all spring to life. Video games were paused, debates were left in abeyance, beers were put down unfinished. Throwing up the blinds and opening the windows, we would wait, silently enduring the sun on our skin and cold central New York air

I Love Charts

in our lungs. When the tour had safely passed our dorm (for though our intentions were courageous, our modus operandi was cowardice), we would all take a deep breath and scream, "Come to Hamilton!" before diving back to the safety of the floor and anonymity.

I know now that we were wrong about a lot back then. We were politicians trying to regulate the Internet—we understood way less then we claimed to know. Time adds perspective and from where I now stand, I can tell we were full of it. At least now I've learned enough to suspect that I know nothing at all. When I look back, I rarely think about *what* we talked about. We pettifogged over plenty of perfectly pointless practices and parables. I never wonder what we said, but I do wonder about the people who heard us. Particularly those prospective students.

Think of all those kids, trying to sift through it all in a weekend. Was there ever anyone who heard us and in that moment made up their mind one way or the other? A student who heard our cries and succumbed to peer pressure? Someone whose future was altered by our questionably genuine advice?

It seems crazy, right? Who would take the advice of a disembodied shout? Although, we all do get advice from the weirdest places. Sometimes I base decisions on logic, but sometimes I base them on common cents. Heads. Tails. Washington. Washington. Eagle. You've got to trust something, so maybe it is better a strange Samaritan than an anonymous alloy tumbling through the atmosphere. Like the universe has your back. Not that old yarn. I'd rather trust strangers than fiction.

I did a brief stint working in a vitamin shop. You know: meatheads, melatonin, and me. No whey, José: pro teens and biotics. A weird place to work from alpha to omega 3. Men with bodies like inverted potted plants; all soil and substance up top resting on tiny twigs below. Get fit fast? Hell, get fit with speed, that's essentially what it was.

Stranger still than testosterone pills was a stranger's trust. People asked me for advice all the time. Maybe my idiolect implies candor, maybe my smile is free of rancor. Maybe it was just that I was wearing a tie, but people trusted me. Me. The guy behind the counter. I might as well have been in a three-piece on the back of a wagon.

"Gather round! Gather round! Try our new snake oil elixir, straight from the Orient! Gives you the strength of ten men. Used topically, it will cure any rash; used industrially, it will unstick any axle or hinge!"

Me, selling magic beans for cash cows. Me, a Nigerian prince in need. But people took my word as gospel. All I did was read them exactly what was on the back of the box, but people seemed to instantly put their faith in me.

And I do it too, don't get me wrong, even having been on the other side of the register. I walk into a store and put myself in the possibly capable, probably culpable hands of its employees. I upgrade the memory because the guy with the goatee seems to know what's up. I can get a deluxe set for an extra thirty dollars? It comes with a car charger?! But I don't own a car. What's that? Good point, one day I might; take my money, good sir. I know he's working on commission, but I trust his intuition of what's right for me.

When it comes down to it, we're all self-conscious about making the wrong decisions. Especially when it comes to purchases that other people will see. No one wants to be the kid with the Zune. We're all terrified that if left to our own devices, our tastes will be devastatingly contrary to popular opinion. If all my friends jumped off the Brooklyn Bridge, I may or may not join them, but I certainly wouldn't go jump off the Triboro. Socially speaking, there's safety in numbers. At some point we all realize that there is simply way too much we need to know in order to live comfortably these days, and only the monastic sacrifice succors for self-reliance.

So we put our trust in strangers. We see doctors when things don't feel right in our bodies. We see dentists when things don't feel right in our mouths. We see optometrists once a year just to make sure our eyes aren't failing. Was it scary going blind? Nah, I never saw it coming. Okay, maybe medical professionals merit our trust, but we don't stop there. We talk to the guy at the computer store for two hours, we ask the girl behind the counter if we can pull off this shirt with these pants. We ask coworkers for restaurant recommendations and the wait staff for entrée advice. Some people read advice columns without irony. We're all crazy and scared and looking for a word to point us in the right direction.

Did any of those prospective students ever listen to our advice? Maybe. It's hard to say. But people take advice from stranger places than strangers. Face it, it's more what than who or where. So you can flip a coin or heed the hollers of newborn scholars. You can put your faith in the universe or humanity. But you have to take advice from somewhere if you don't want to go it alone. Reliable? Perhaps. But if you want my advice, you've got to roll the dice and just sit back and see if all works out.

—Cody

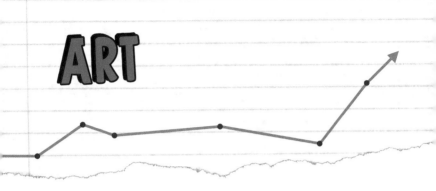

ART

AS WE SAID IN the introduction, our favorite charts deal in qualitative matters, putting them in a quantitative context. There are also many charts that take our breath away with their brilliance while dealing only in the qualitative. There is, however, another type of chart, a chart whose existence is its purpose. These charts are self-aware, recursive, and give the viewer reason to scratch his or her head. These charts make us suspect there is more to come out of this golden age of visualization, a purpose beyond data, lulz, and nerditry. These push the boundaries of what charts can be, and not always with grandiose agenda. Often, they just want to make a joke. Though it may be too broad a term, we refer to these as art charts or chART. We will now let the art speak for itself.

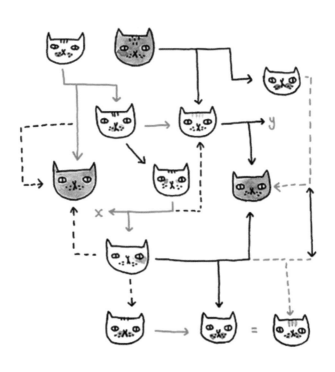

THIS DIAGRAM IS ENTIRELY NONSENSICAL.
BUT LOOK AT ALL THE KITTENS!

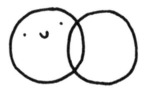

THIS VENN DIAGRAM
DOES NOT MEAN ANYTHING.

BUT IT'S VERY CUTE.

GEMMA CORRELL

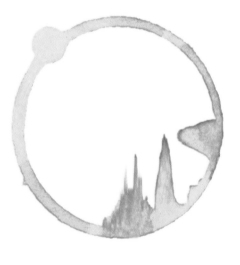

**Percent Done I Was With My Coffee
When I Noticed That It Had Made This Stain**

©2011 Ben Greenman/Stupid Ideas

SCRAPPED CLOCK DESIGN

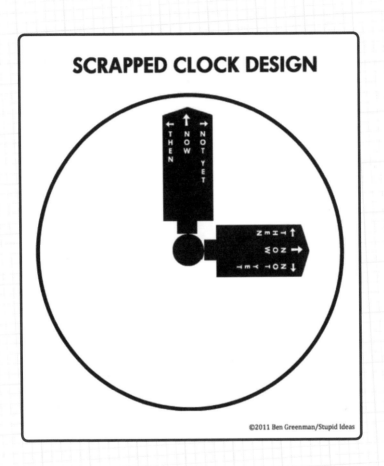

Art

CODY'S QUIP

Do not push it.

If you choose an answer to this question at random, what is the chance you will be correct?

A) 25%   B) 50%

C) 100%   D) 25%

Why I'm Not Where You Are, pt 2
Something and Nothing

something something
we must be murky
eyes that try to see
traces of affection
semblance of connection
something in your feel
framing what is real

heart still beating
something
heating
(don't you know that time is fleeting?)

nothing nothing is routine
past and future are not seen
stories
blind
nothing on my mind
mingling with the truth

silent
in the
light of
fiction
there
arose   a
shade of
friction

n empty youth
nothing
burns **we are not**
yet still we yearn
(this is cause for great concern)

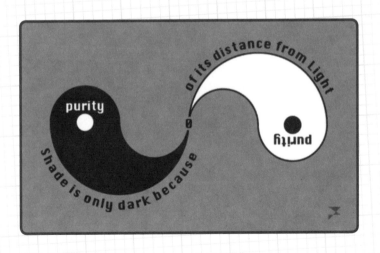

purity

Shade is only dark because

of its distance from Light

purity

I Love Charts

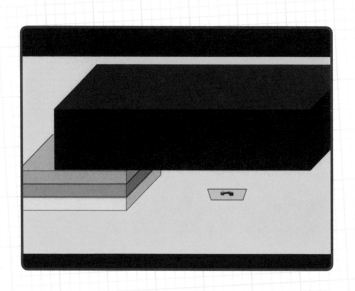

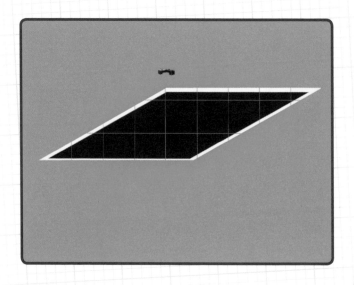

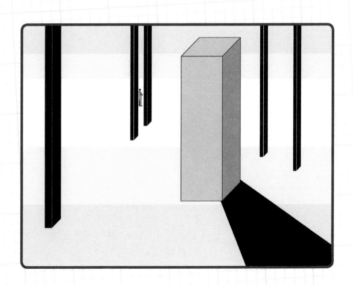

I Love Charts

LOSS

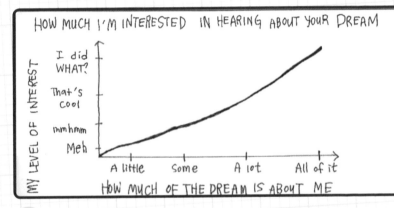

HOW MUCH I'M INTERESTED IN HEARING ABOUT YOUR DREAM

MY LEVEL OF INTEREST

I did WHAT?

That's cool

mmhmm

Meh

A little   Some   A lot   All of it

HOW MUCH OF THE DREAM IS ABOUT ME

Last night I dreamt that my parents and I went on a vacation. In a process that seemed quite natural, we paid for transport back in time to the 1950s. I sat down by a window in the living room of the house I grew up in. The house moved.

When we arrived, I saw from out my window a Kennedy brother jump up and grasp a rope ladder attached to a zeppelin taking off from our yard. My ears were packed with white noise. I was now on the lawn watching the zeppelin wobble, but elevate.

The Kennedy, in a gray suit and tie, hung by one hand, the other limp by his side. I was worried for his safety, but he called out, beaming, "It's alright! I'll be fine; I'm a Kennedy!" That voice and those crow's feet were reassuring.

The zeppelin rose beyond my ability to make out the

Kennedy, so I moved to a perspective parallel to him, floating alongside the rope ladder. My ears cleared. His chestnut side part allowed the wind to displace it, and it moved like an animal released. The sun was setting and had reached an angle where it was directly in his eyes. He dug his crow's feet deeper, which made him seem slightly manic. He did not know I was there alongside him.

Above us, in the basket of the zeppelin, another brother, older and wider, was grappling with a young blonde in a bikini. He appeared to be laughing, but I could not hear. I did not see her face. He managed to lock his hands around her forearms and swung her legs over the side of the basket. All high heels and white legs, which were almost too bright to look at, time dialed back its pace with her arc over the railing, the elder Kennedy the center of the circle, and the point of her heel cutting a circumference in the cornflower sky. She swung half a circle off the edge, then I lost sight of her and returned to my perspective at the living room window.

It was raining and venetian red outside. I tried to hide tears. My parents occasionally approached me but I would stand and change windows, and with each move the tears came with more force. At the fourth window, my mother reached for my shoulder, made contact, and I could hold back no longer.

Outside, my yard was no different than it is currently constructed, yet was chopped into alternating sheets of rain and red. I told my mother and my sisters (who had now arrived, one telling the other not to change any numbers she saw written anywhere for fear of cosmic consequences), that I wanted to do nothing other than travel backward in time. I wasn't sure if it was to mourn or to learn.

I was running around the intersection of Massachusetts Avenue and Mt. Auburn Street in Cambridge, staring at strangers' faces and straining to fix their features in my mind, knowing that with the effort of increased perception I was dangerously close to forcing myself awake. I could feel my (real) eyes. I told my family, between spasms of perspective shifts and flashes of young

I Love Charts

Kennedy boys chasing a dog across a manicured New England lawn, that the hard part was knowing everything here was dead.

Actually, everything was not dead, but rather would die. In that, there was nothing different from every storm, sensation, and cataloged feature of the present. My eyes opened and everything was dark.

—Jason

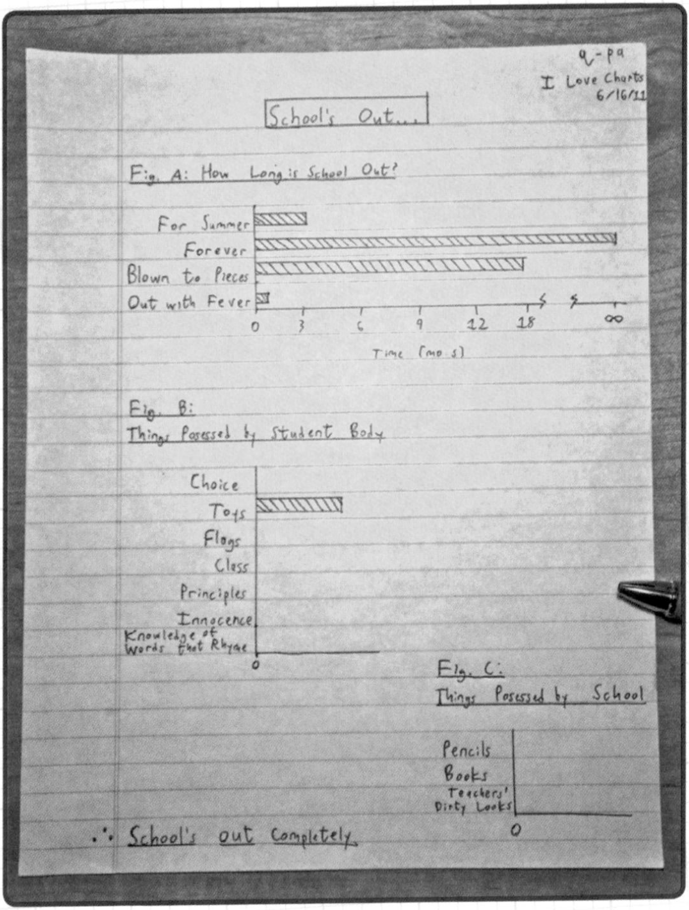

q-pa
I Love Charts
6/16/11
School's Out...
Fig. A: How Long is School Out?
For Summer
Forever
Blown to Pieces
Out with Fever
0
3
6
9
12
18
∞
Time (mo.s)
Fig. B:
Things Posessed by Student Body
Choice
Toys
Flags
Class
Principles
Innocence
Knowledge of Words that Rhyme
0
Fig. C:
Things Posessed by School
Pencils
Books
Teachers' Dirty Looks
0
∴ School's out completely.

SO, WHAT IS THE future of charts? The simple answer is, whatever people need it to be. Charts are tools for communication and are proving themselves widely adaptable to that end. The "final frontier" of charts lies with those who care about them, who use them to express their hopes, fears, humorous observations, and inspiration. The art form will go as far as our imagination allows it.

In that spirit, this final chapter is comprised of charts created by the Tumblr community. Their imagination has made the blog what it is today, and will no doubt carry us to a bright chart-riddled future. These are our favorite homemade follower submissions from the last two-and-a-half years.

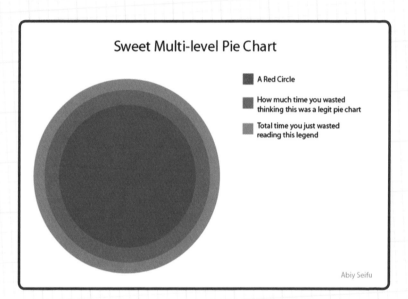

I Love Charts

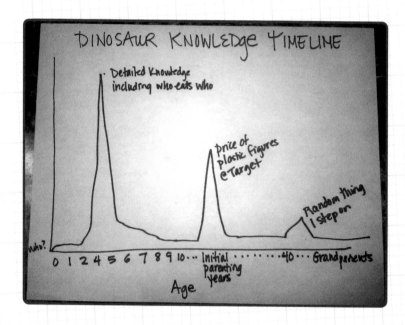

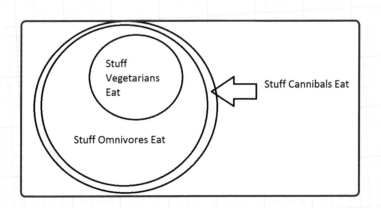

Stuff Vegetarians Eat

Stuff Cannibals Eat

Stuff Omnivores Eat

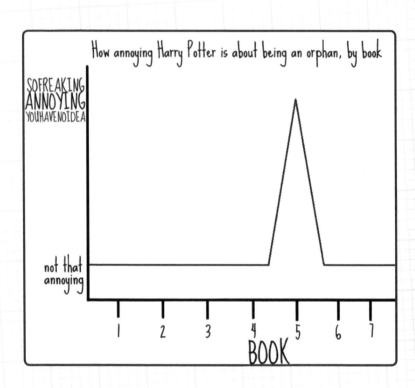

I Love Charts

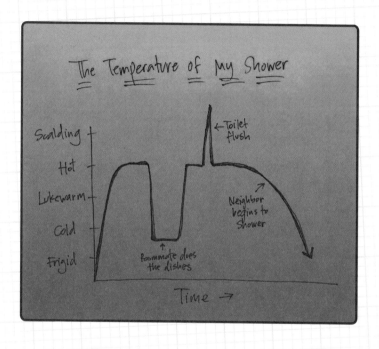

Places I put my drink first

Places I put my drink second

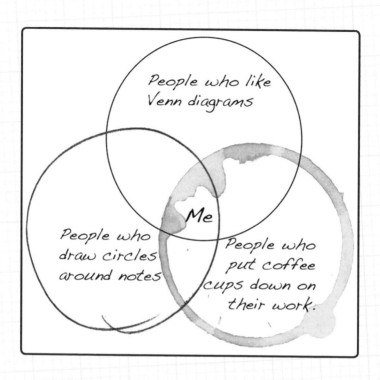

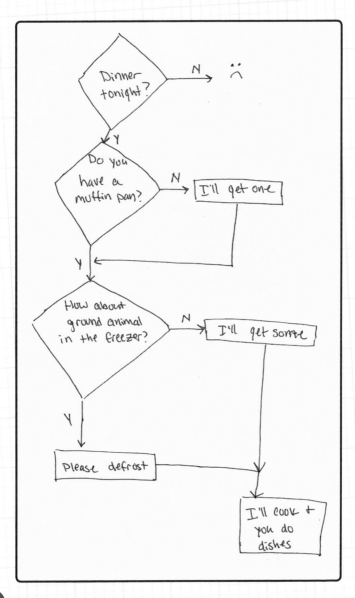

I Love Charts

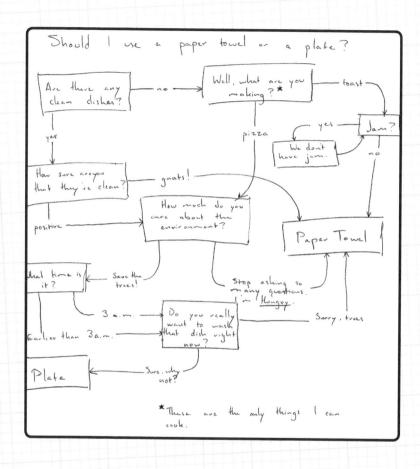

Should I use a paper towel or a plate?

Are there any clean dishes? —no→ Well, what are you making? ✱ —toast→

↓ yes

How sure are you that they're clean? —gnats!→

positive →

pizza ↓

How much do you care about the environment?

Jam? —yes→ We don't have jam.

Jam? —no→

Paper Towel

What time is it? ←Save the trees!—

3 a.m. → Do you really want to wash that dish right now?

Earlier than 3a.m. →

Stop asking so many questions. I'm _Hungry_. →

Sorry, trees →

Plate ←Sure, why not?—

✱ These are the only things I can cook.

Imagination 129

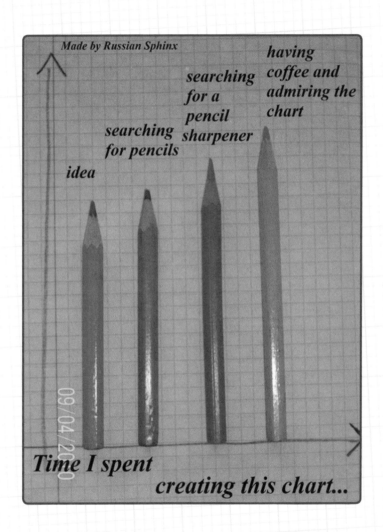

Things that need to be done, bought, or researched...and need funding

Things that can be covered with available funding

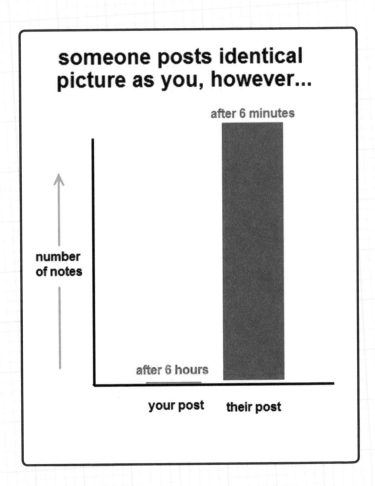

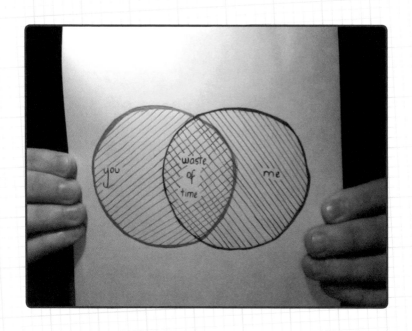

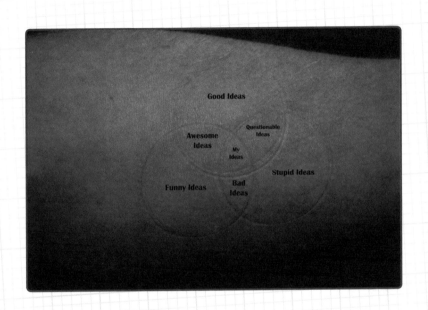

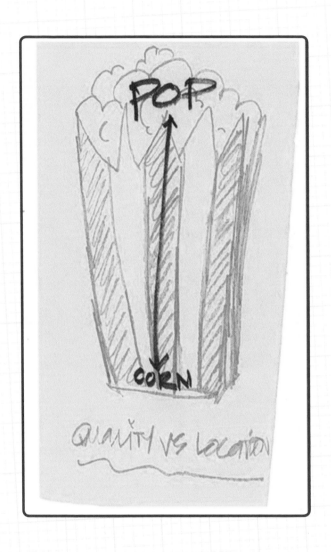

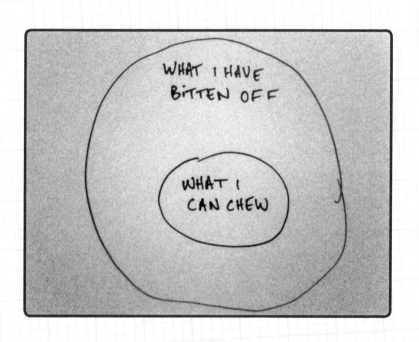

I Love Charts

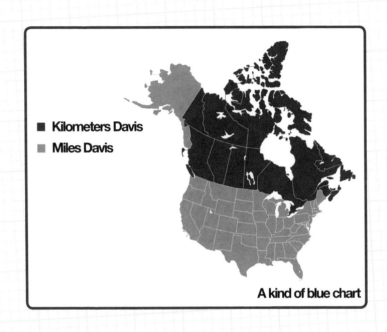

- **Kilometers Davis**
- **Miles Davis**

A kind of blue chart

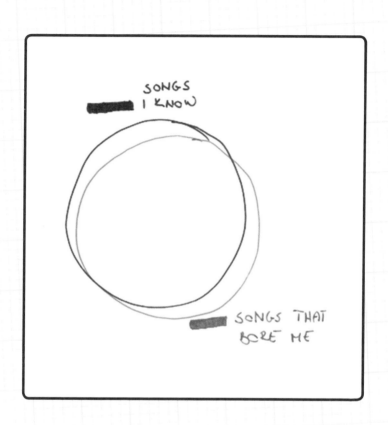

I Love Charts

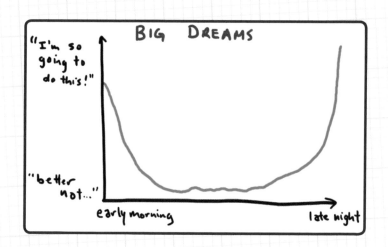

I Love Charts

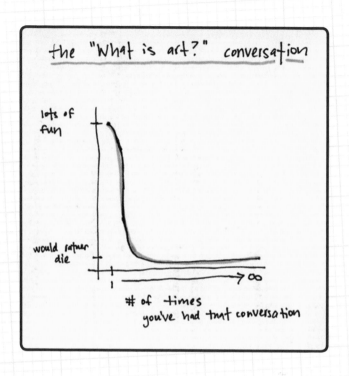

the "What is art?" conversation

lots of fun

would rather die

# of times
you've had that conversation

1 → ∞

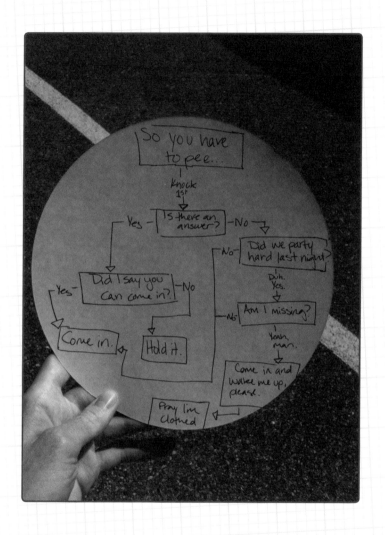

I Love Charts

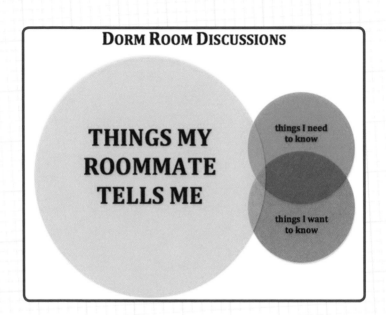

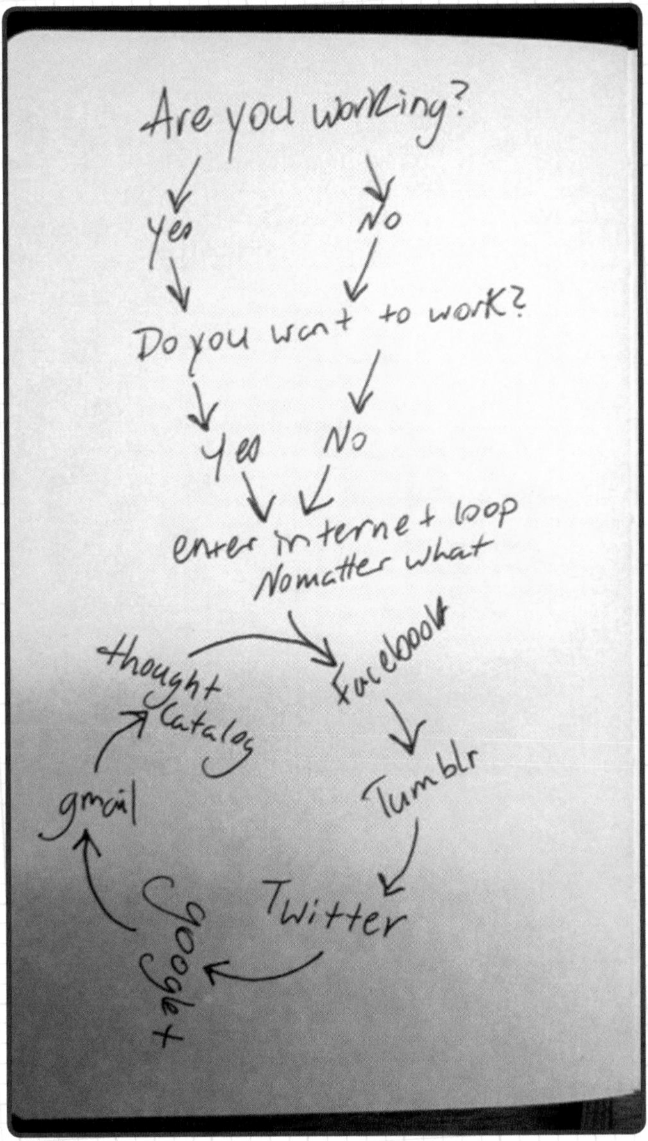

Are you working?

Yes → No

Yes → Do you want to work?

Yes → No

enter internet loop
No matter what

thought Catalog → facebook → Tumblr → Twitter → google → gmail

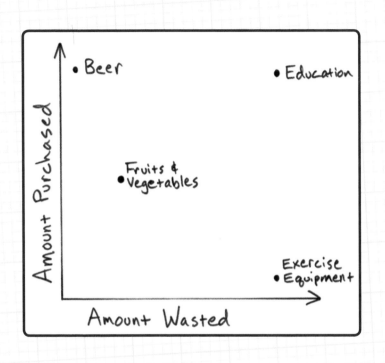

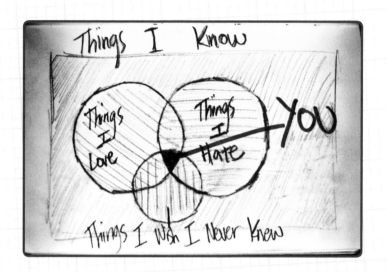

I Love Charts

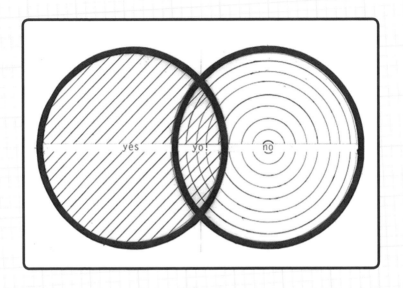

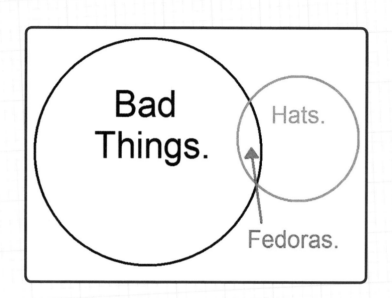

I Love Charts

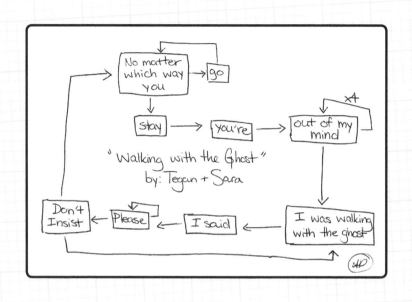

"Walking with the Ghost"
by: Tegan + Sara

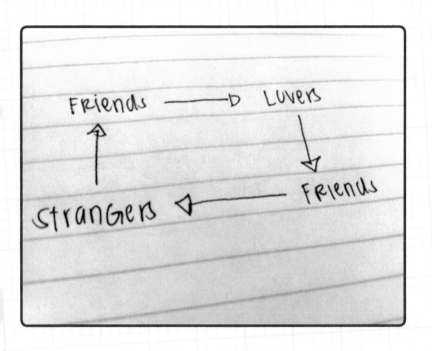

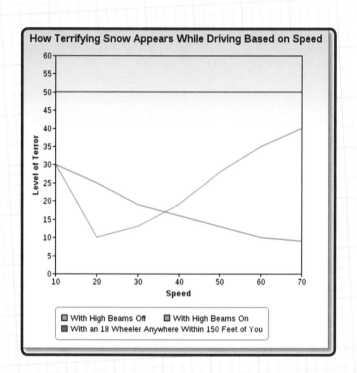

I Love Charts

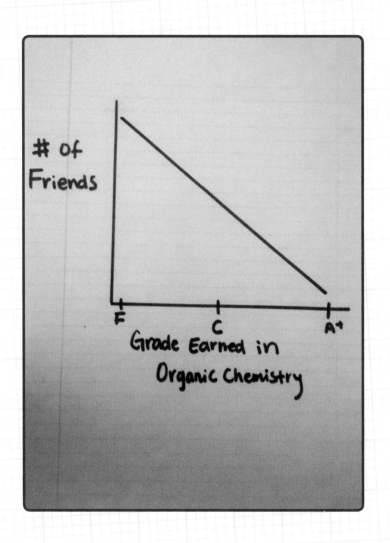

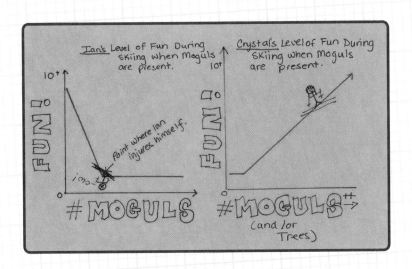

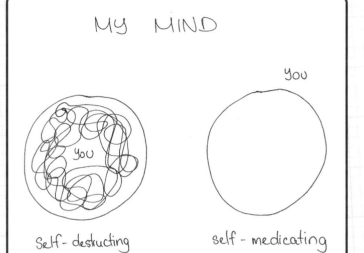

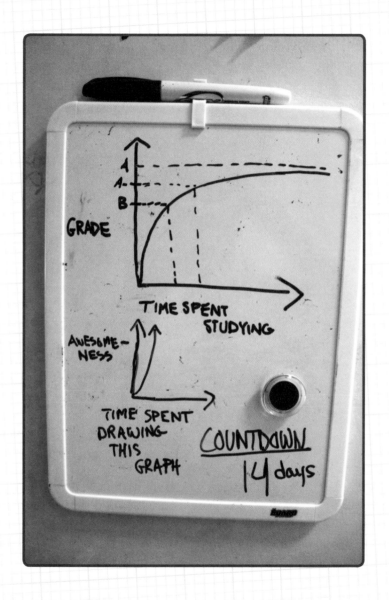

I Love Charts

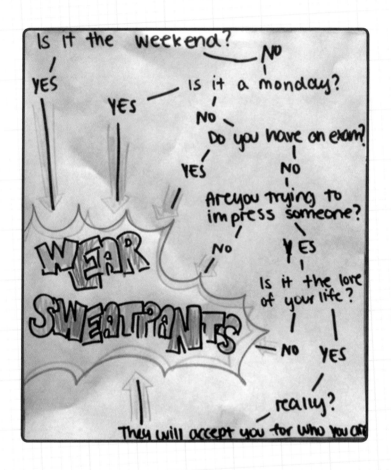

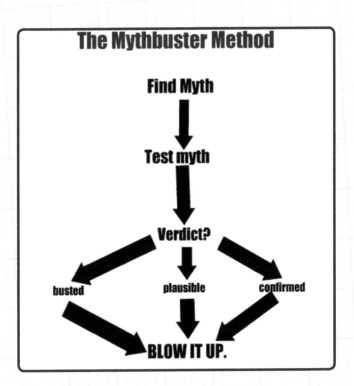

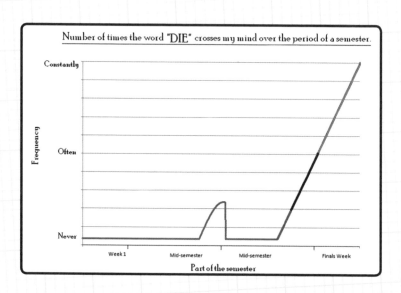

Number of times the word "DIE" crosses my mind over the period of a semester.

I Love Charts

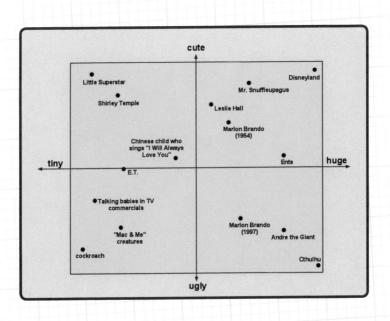

cute

Little Superstar

Disneyland

Mr. Snuffleupagus

Shirley Temple

Leslie Hall

Marlon Brando
(1954)

Chinese child who
sings "I Will Always
Love You"

tiny

Ents

huge

E.T.

Talking babies in TV
commercials

Marlon Brando
(1997)

"Mac & Me"
creatures

Andre the Giant

cockroach

Cthulhu

ugly

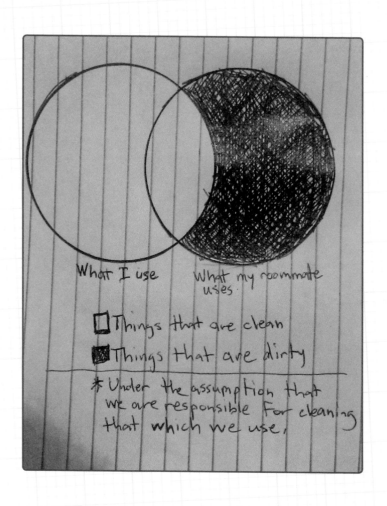

What I use

What my roommate uses.

☐ Things that are clean

■ Things that are dirty

* Under the assumption that we are responsible for cleaning that which we use.

I Love Charts

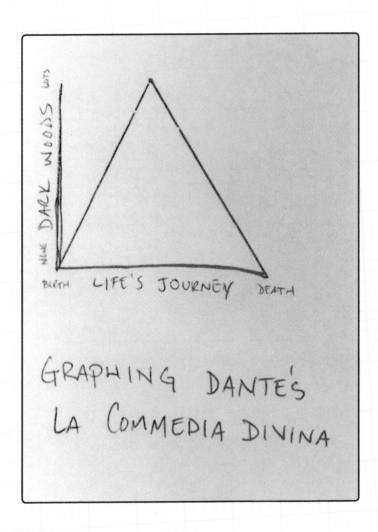

GRAPHING DANTE'S
LA COMMEDIA DIVINA

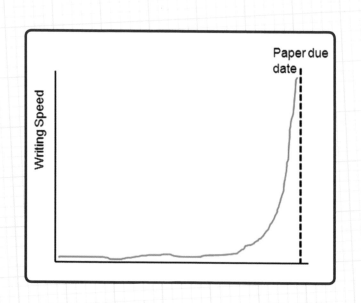

I Love Charts

$\frac{1}{2}$ air

$\frac{1}{2}$ water

technically, on an atomic level, the glass is mostly empty.

I Love Charts

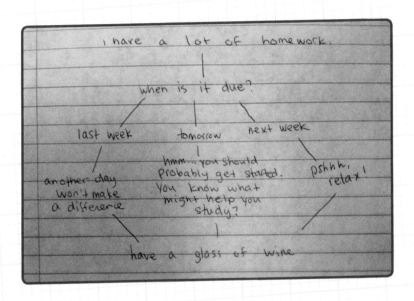

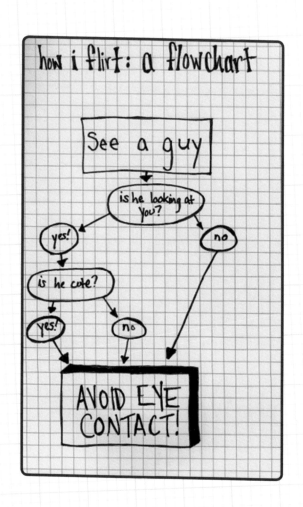

I Love Charts

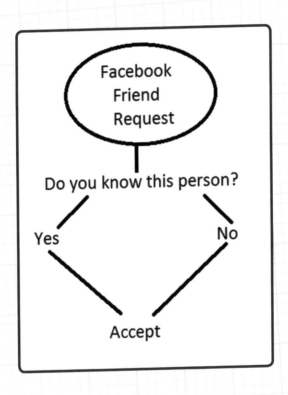

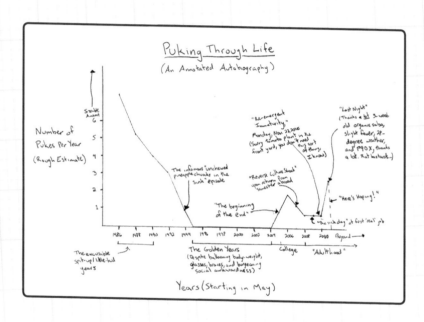

I Love Charts

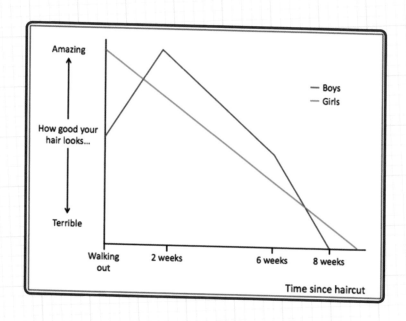

I Love Charts

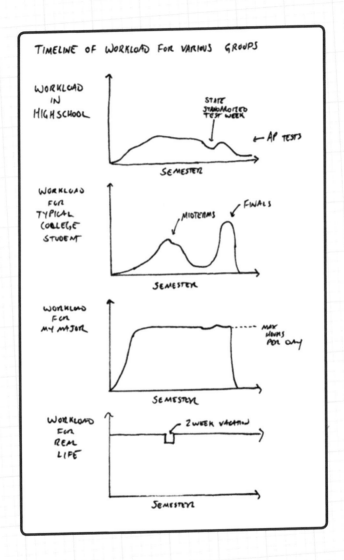

TIMELINE OF WORKLOAD FOR VARIOUS GROUPS

WORKLOAD IN HIGH SCHOOL

STATE STANDARDIZED TEST WEEK

← AP TESTS

SEMESTER

WORKLOAD FOR TYPICAL COLLEGE STUDENT

MIDTERMS

FINALS

SEMESTER

WORKLOAD FOR MY MAJOR

MAX HOURS PER DAY

SEMESTER

WORKLOAD FOR REAL LIFE

2 WEEK VACATION

SEMESTER

Imagination 173

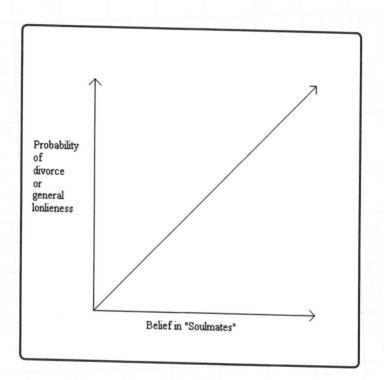

I Love Charts

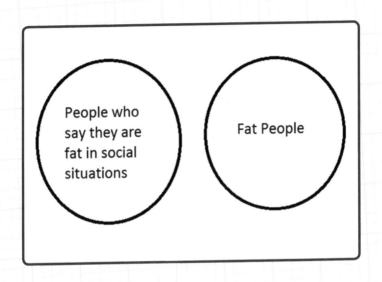

People who say they are fat in social situations

Fat People

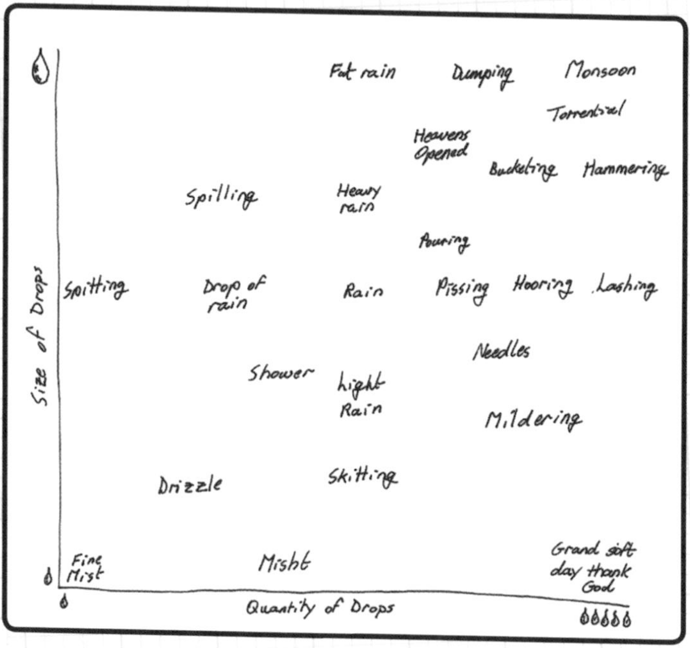
Fat rain
Dumping
Monsoon
Torrential
Heavens Opened
Bucketing
Hammering
Spilling
Heavy rain
Pouring
Spitting
Drop of rain
Rain
Pissing
Hooring
Lashing
Needles
Shower
Light Rain
Mildering
Drizzle
Skitting
Fine Mist
Misht
Grand soft day thank God
Size of Drops
Quantity of Drops

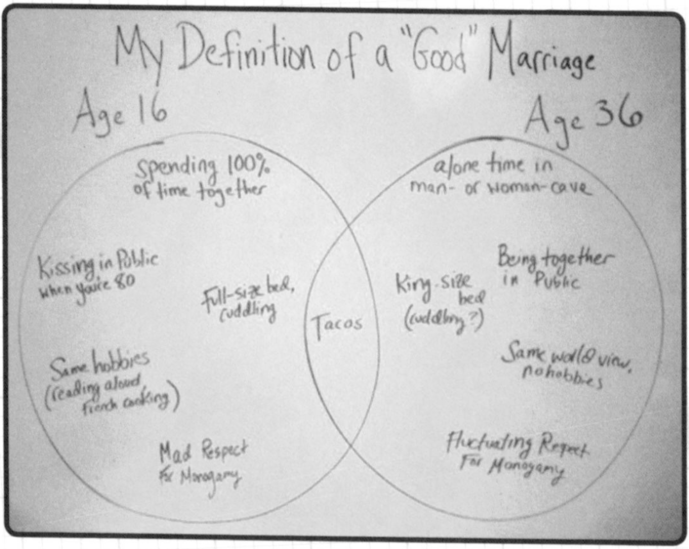

My Definition of a "Good" Marriage

Age 16

Age 36

Spending 100% of time together

alone time in man- or woman-cave

Kissing in Public when you're 80

Full-size bed, cuddling

King-size bed (cuddling?)

Being together in Public

Tacos

Same hobbies (reading aloud, French cooking)

Same world view, no hobbies

Mad Respect For Monogamy

Fluctuating Respect For Monogamy

PEOPLE'S REACTION UPON LEARNING I'M AN ENGLISH MAJOR

- What do you do, exactly?

- Pssh, my parents wouldn't pay for college if I was an English major.
- So...you're going to be a teacher?

- I hate reading.

- It's great that you're doing something that you love!

Imagination

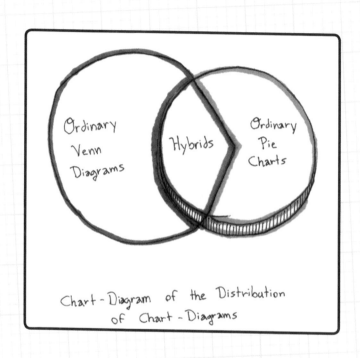

Chart - Diagram of the Distribution
of Chart - Diagrams

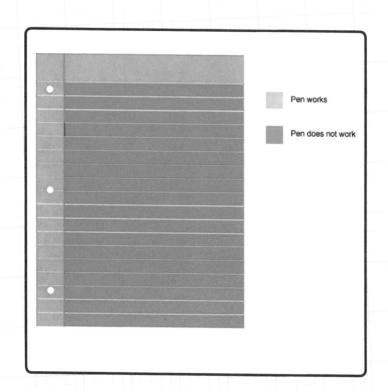

Pen works

Pen does not work

I Love Charts

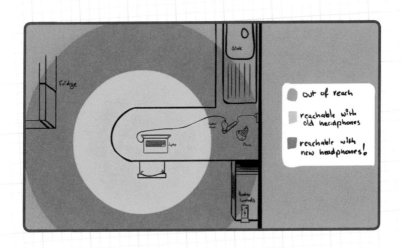

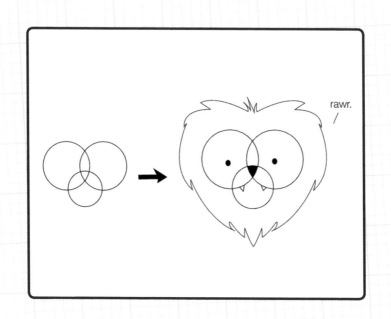

rawr.

FAREWELL

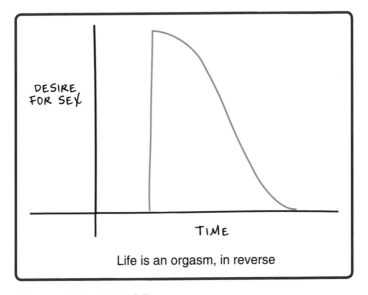

Life is an orgasm, in reverse

WELL, HERE WE ARE at the end. If we haven't yet convinced you we are qualified to write this book, you should
probably buy a copy for a friend and have them read it. They

will probably be able to help you see what you are missing. If they have the same trouble you are having, buy a copy for another friend. Continue until you run out of friends or money.

If we *have* convinced you we are qualified to write this book and you enjoyed it, remember that the world may be ending this year, which means you should buy a friend a copy of this book sooner rather than later. Continue until you run out of friends or money, or the world ends.

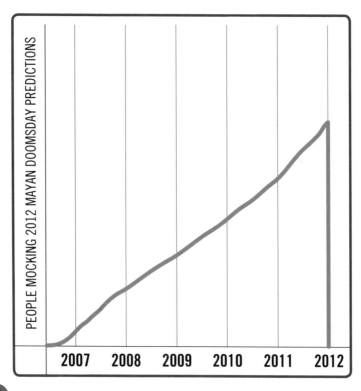

I Love Charts

We would like to thank all the absurdly talented people featured in this book for their contributions. They inspire us and entertain us and are just generally awesome people.

$$(A > B) = \text{Stagnation}$$

$$(A = B) = \text{Implementation}$$

$$A = \text{Reality}$$

$$B = \text{Ideas}$$

$$(A < B) = \text{Imagination}$$

Finally, we would like to thank all our followers on Tumblr, especially anybody who has ever submitted a chart. You teach us, inspire us, make us laugh and grimace and occasionally get a little misty. You are the reason we could do this and the reason we still love charts.

Hugs and hand-pounds,
Jason & Cody

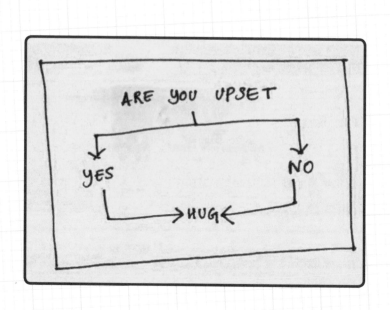

I Love Charts

CHART CREDITS

adisasterpiece: 131

aisthetes: 132

Alderson, Bruce (robotpony): 34, 75

alexbowler: 133

Anabelle: 121

Anjarwalla, Tasneem (postgradlife): 28

Ansari, Sahifah (athoreauinvestigation):
26, 30

Anthoni (amorilinguae): 72

armlost: 134

arnndffr: 162

Atcheson, Jordan (stained-class): 110

bcauseyes: 135

Bencista, Giacomo (f-featherbrain): 17

Bisson, Martino (brothermartino): 83

braiker: 136

Chris, Buddy: 122

Correll, Gemma: 8, 104, 105

Crowe, Scotty: 13, 47, back cover

DeLucia, Nico (Endless Origami): 10, 67,
96

Digginginthedirt: 137

dorka: 138

Drankwalter, Dannie: 109

Duncanson, Paul: 127

ebecks: 139

Ells, Laura (lauraells): 76

emilysayshi: 141

Fee, Toby: 89

Fernando, Lambert: 113

fishfingersandcumberbatch: 142

Flaherty, Scott (justfakeit): 170

funnifications: 143

genesse: 144

geniuspending: 145

Gilliland, Kendall Bouldin (This is Not That
Blog): 6, 62, 90, back cover

Gocklin, Stephanie (stephemera): 90, 94

Green, Walter (waltergreens): 48, 49, 50,
51

Greenman, Ben (New Yorker): 106, 107,
108

greenpants: 146

Grelle, Ben (The Frogman): xiv

Hackett, Phil (xwidep): 46, 108

Hagy, Jessica (Indexed): 33, 63, 187

hellohellophant: 147

Hoang, Nathan (The Moosehead): xvi

ihatefedoras: 148
imdressedlikeavulcan: 149
imyourguy: 150
ishanow: 151
isthisyournikki: 152
itsdash: 153
itsfuntopokeeyes: 154
Jill's 5th graders: 124
johnsanchez: 161
Johnson, Ben (clockworkgrue): v
Johnstone, Mark (Epic Graph): x
KAC: 125
kerenrohe: 156
klazar: 157
Krishnan, Madhura (bandragirl): 15, 43, 188
LaRue, John (tdylf): 64, 65
Lee, Dami (As Per Usual): 11, 114, 115
Lewy, Michael: 111, 112
Luong, Eric (ehalcyon): 110, 139
Melick, Angela (Wasted Talent): 60
menstrom: 158
Mex: 126
Miller, Mary (ratsoff): 53
moniquey: 159
mosessumney: 160
Nafziger, Jason (rockcharts): 88, 90, 92, 93
nhoe: 155
nickseam: 163
Nicolet, Jesse (stuffistolefromtheinternet): 186
nzatodaklop: 164
oatmealandbears: 165
pablopistachio: 166
padialogue: 167
Pampena, Simon: 87
Parshall, Jordan (jpjoj): 73

partylikeazombie: 168
perfect1n54n17y: 169
Pope, Dan: 86
progressivedance: 171
q-pa: 118
rdeeming: 172
reductoabsurdum: 173
Reese Rackets: 147
reidev275: 174
Russian Sphinx: 130
Seifu, Abiy Z: 120
Sharp, Greg (Complicated Shoes): XIII, 37
sheissofedorable: 175
Shepherd, Dante (Surviving the World): 23, 44, 78, 84
sliabh (dot) net: 176
spacecowboywhit: 177
spousonomics: 178
starsburnforit: 179
Steele, Emily (Figment): 123
Sundquist, Josh: 5, 9, 95
Tang, Yau Hoong: 74, back cover
taylorhasa: 180
Tipsy & Pongoo (Googly Gooeys): 3, 12
tiptopgash: 181
Venot, Rebecca: 128
wallowinginmyownselfcreys: 182
webbot15: 183
Weiner, Zach (Saturday Morning Breakfast Cereal): xi, 31, 54, 69, 185
Westphal, Cody: ix, 14, 25, 29, 32, 45, 52, 68, 85, 105
Wysaski, Jeff (Pleated Jeans): 21, 35, 36, 55
zhaliang: 184

About the Authors

JASON OBERHOLTZER AND **CODY WESTPHAL** created the blog *I Love Charts* in September of 2009 for themselves and their friends. In the two-and-a-half years since, the site has grown exponentially to more than 100,000 followers on Tumblr, 20,000 on Twitter, and more than half a million page views a month. They live near New York City, New York.